Joanna
604 767 4773

One must still have chaos in oneself to give birth to a dancing star.

FRIEDRICH NIETZSCHE, *Thus Spoke Zarathustra*

Some names and identifying characteristics of individuals mentioned have been changed to protect their privacy.

Contents

III. The Mama Blues 129

IV. The Whole Mom 179

The Mother Trip

Preface: Chaos Training

It will be a sore fight letting go and letting the sea in.
JOANNA FIELD, *A Life of One's Own*

We have children because mothering is good for the soul. Having kids won't make us rich. It won't make our lives more tranquil. We do it because it's good for the soul. Simple, right? But motherhood is never simple. Because we don't just get new people to raise when we become mama-women. No, with them come all the chaos of personal transformation and a wicked little cultural blueprint for soul-sacrifice and depression cleverly disguised as helpful advice and "what's best for the children."

Here we thought we'd come so far—survived our girlhoods, revived Ophelia, embraced our inner dorks, declared ourselves to the world as whole and independent women— and then we wake up in the middle of one night, exhausted and horrified, with a newborn or a brood of rug rats, wondering what on earth we've gotten ourselves into. And we can hardly help but wonder: *Maybe Dan Quayle had it right all along.*

❖

American families have always been incredibly diverse. We all know that. We also know that Grandma Lulu was propped up on Valium and Grandma Millie worked three jobs. It's not the past we feel suddenly nostalgic for. It's more like an apple-pie-in-the-sky perfect-mother perfect-family fantasy kind of thing that can—especially when we're tired—be incredibly seductive. It tells us what our families should look like. It tells us who we should be and how we should act. It promises stability, eternal happiness and laundry that's whiter than white.

The modern mama fantasy includes layers of the 1980s Super Mom, the 1950s happy housewife, the early twentieth-century domestic scientist and the Victorian fountain of moral purity. Underneath all that there's the flickering memory of slavery, genocide and some three hundred years of witch hunts when we burned our midwives and our wise women at the stake and women's real lives became the stuff of secrets.

When we have kids, we can't help but catch a glimpse of that old knowledge buried under all our cultural fantasies. We see the personal transformation we've signed up for in its full chaotic glory and too often, because we're also exhausted and hopelessly unsupported, we get scared. So, like our mothers and grandmothers before us, we back away from the soulful transformation and instead take the blueprint and start selling off pieces of our soul for those weird promises of stability.

To varying extents, we all do it. As the Buddhist nun Pema Chödrön says, "Fear is a natural reaction to moving closer to the truth." But our flight into those empty promises is the reason mothers are the most depressed segment of the American population. There's no such thing as whiter than white. We all know that. And the alternative to chaos isn't stability—it's psychic death.

My friend Wendy describes the Pacific as a vast ocean of mothers' tears. "How sad!" I blurted out as we sat drinking lattes at Royal Coffee. But she shook her head: "It's not sad." Motherhood is not what we imagined. It is more delightful, more heartbreaking. It ruins everything. It's not the calm after the storm we have been led to expect. It is almost more than a person can bear. *Almost.*

The German translation of the title of my first book, *The Hip Mama Survival Guide,* is *Chaostraining Rund Ums Kind.* Chaos Training. How right on is that? The word *chaos* brings up images of disorder, confusion and turmoil. But modern chaos theory doesn't claim that there's no order in the universe. No, chaos theory just reminds us that the order is intricate and changeable, that we might as well just give up trying to control and predict things. It's the scientific version of "do your best and forget the rest."

Only chaos theory can explain a dripping water faucet, the branches of a tree, blood vessels, the beat of a human heart, my desk or the nature of motherhood. Because it's change at work here. Chaos is reality. It's truth. So the next time anybody tries to sell you stability, make sure you don't get suckered into paying too dearly for it. It's a junk bond. It's whiter than white. Apple-pie-in-the-sky, big patriarchal lie. If that weren't bummer enough, it's also more toxic than three Big Macs and a Prozac shake. The more of it you eat, the sicker you'll feel.

Over the holidays last winter, I put my writing and editing life aside to take a temporary job wrapping gifts at a local independent bookstore. And since all of about six people wanted me to wrap their books, I took the opportunity to read all the books that shared the parenting section with my own. A few were lovely reads. But as you can imagine, I also endured some fascist tomes. I learned it was best to breast-feed and better to bottle-feed. I learned that if I put an infant on an abusively rigid feeding schedule, I could induce sleep. I learned that in some cultures the pregnant and postpartum body is considered sacred, and I learned that fifty sit-ups, fifty push-ups, fifty jumping jacks and a lap around the block between diaper changes would go a long way to making *my* body sacred. I learned that I alone was responsible for the mental and physical well-being of my kid and I learned that if I needed help I could pretty well just go shoot myself in the head. I read a hundred pieces of conflicting advice from hack psychologists, but the clearest, most consistent message was this: Withhold all of your own knowledge, Mom, and follow *my* rules. To quote from the modern parenting manual *On Becoming Babywise*, "Feelings are not and never will be the basis of sound decision-making. Why would intuition suddenly assume center stage in this, [a woman's] most critical role?"

Scary.

I remember reading a story somewhere about a medical student who had been quite gifted in the healing arts. As a resident, however, he was taught to be exhausted. He noticed that the less sleep he got, the more tests he had to order. Where he had once ordered tests only to confirm his intuition, he was now so exhausted he couldn't tap his intuition! He was just shooting in the dark—gimme some X-rays, a biopsy . . . maybe an *advice* book.

This really is what they're trying to feed us: "Feelings are not and never will be the basis of sound decision making." I may not be able to find the words to describe how deeply I understood our predicament after reading that declaration. It crystalized for me in the form of a circular equation that looked something like this:

Exhaustion + Bad Advice
=
Dependence on Bad Advice
No Access to Intuition
=
Increased Exhaustion
Knowledge Withheld
=
Depression

As a parenting writer, I've been told by more editors than I'd like to remember to dumb down my ideas. "Mainstream mothers won't understand this," they tell me. But I've met too many of my readers to be fooled by such nonsense. Many of you understand more than I—and none of you has ever asked me to "dumb it down." And why would you? Did you check your personality at the maternity-ward door? Did you go to sleep on your first kid's birthday and wake, as if from a dream, having forgotten who you were and all you knew? If so, we've got to go back and *get* your personality. We've got to remember. We don't have to dumb anything down.

Our intuition isn't always accessible. We need each other's support and helpful words. What we don't need is junk-food advice that tells us to ignore our feelings, that undermines our confidence and insults our intelligence. It's just a recipe for depression. Because what is intuition? It's a capacity of the spirit. It's knowledge. And what is depression? It's low spirits. It's knowledge withheld. But there is also a jumping-off point from this circular equation, a point where we can recognize our exhaustion for what it is, give ourselves a break, and in that quiet hour begin to transform the energy our culture has taught us to use to scrutinize and blame ourselves, and turn it outward, into something revolutionary.

This book is an attempt to chronicle, in real time, my own trip out of the depression equation. I wrote the stories and essays in it over a three-year period. I'd been traveling around talking to lots of moms, thinking about the realities of motherhood and the layers of fantasy we've built into the work of raising kids. I wanted to explore how we can continue to reject the cultural blueprint we've been handed. Because we may know better by now, but I think we are still having a hard time letting go and letting the sea in. I think we are still allowing ourselves to get seduced by promises of tranquility and "happily ever after." And I think we are still blaming ourselves when those promises turn out to be empty. We can withhold our knowledge, it's true. We can juggle, run in circles, we can make ourselves manic, burned out, bummed. But here's the thing: Chaos comes anyway. It comes whether we want it to or not. It comes even if we pretend we don't see it coming. And here's the other thing: Chaos is good news. It's movement. It's change. It's revolution. It's scary. But like intuition, I think we can trust it.

—At home
Early summer, 1999

Forget the Rules

Stop being holy, forget being prudent,
It'll be a hundred times better for everyone.
Stop being altruistic, forget being righteous,
people will remember what family feeling is.
Stop planning, forget making a profit,
there won't be any thieves and robbers.

But even these three rules
Needn't be followed; what works reliably
is to know the raw silk,
hold the uncut wood.
Need little,
want less.
Forget the rules.
Be untroubled.
> —LAO TZU, *Tao Te Ching*, "Raw Silk and Uncut Wood"

Coming Undone

The first night of Maia's life, I thought I would come completely undone. We were in the hospital in the little Italian town where she was born, me laid up in a narrow bed and wrapped in crisp white sheets, she resting in a tiny wheeled metal bassinet, positioned so that I could reach her easily even though I couldn't move the lower half of my body. Every hour the bells of the great church in the town square outside our window sounded, and the entire building shook. In the first hours, I counted the bells. Eleven, then one for the half-hour, then twelve, then one, then one again—and again. . . . Every half-hour the church bells woke the baby. She cried a soft, fussy, animal, newborn cry. I sat up a little, exhausted, would begin to cry with her, then begin to laugh. What was this twisted science experiment we'd become the subject of? I lifted her out of her metal crib and tried to nurse her, rock her, comfort her, whisper mother sounds. But as she fell back asleep, I had to set her down again. My bed seemed too small for the both of us. By the time the church clock sounded 2:00 A.M., my hospital bed had become a lifeboat, floating on foreign seas. I thought I was Max, traveling to "where the wild things are," and I tried to remember just how the story went. By first glassy blue morning light, we had reached the shore of a strange island. The dark ravens that had flown politely back and forth outside our window all through my labor were perched at the end of our lifeboat. And the church bells sounded once more, but this time endlessly, marking no time, just sounding and sounding and sounding, shaking the whole island with their vibrations and causing great waves to swell up in the sea.

Who a Mother "Should" Be

Take a moment to imagine the perfect mother. What does she look like? How does she dress? What does she sound like? Does she wear perfume? What kind? Is she anything like you?

The world tells us all—in a thousand ways—that we are not enough for our kids. The world tells us we are too permissive, too controlling, too chaotic, too old, too young, too square, too whacked, too poor, too extravagant and everything in between.

Serious debates in Congress center on "how to punish the parents without hurting the children." Punish us for what? For being human, usually. As mothers, especially as new mothers, short on sleep and the tenuous confidence that comes with experience, it's easy to slip into believing those voices.

I've accepted a thousand thank-yous from moms who say mine was the only voice of support they heard in a choir of discouragement. "It's so hard to be told over and over that I am unworthy," one mom said after a talk I gave recently.

"I know," I told her. But she didn't believe me. She thought, as we all sometimes do, that she was alone. She thought someone like me—someone who had spent the better part of her life as a mom fighting those voices of discouragement—would be immune to the power of "shoulds." But how could I be?

Have I ever ignored my daughter because I was too busy writing about effective parenting? Have I ever done what might be considered an eccentric proportion of my grocery shopping at 7-Eleven? Have I ever uttered a hurtful word? Morphed into an overprotective Bigfoot mama? Served empty calories for dinner? I have. Of course I have.

When Maia was a baby I had to write one of those "Who am I?" essays college freshmen are forever being asked to produce. In it I wrote about my new motherhood:

I am caught between the tides, between moons new and old . . . caught somewhere between who I am, who I have been, and who I think a mother should be, who I should be . . . I feel too young, feel that I should be more together if I'm going to be a mother, that I should be able to offer something more, that I am not enough, and yet wanting to be honest . . .

I was embarrassed when I got to class and heard the other essays—the ones by upbeat, childless eighteen-year-olds that said, "I am an environmentalist" or "I love to swim" or "I am an Italian American." But even then I knew this feeling of being caught between the tides, between who I was and who the world tells us a mother should be, was significant.

Back then I felt I "should" be more together, and over the years I have been able to fill in the blank with dozens of other things I have felt, or heard, I "should" be.

I have felt, and been told, that I have blown it as a mother a thousand times: by having Maia too young, not having enough money, having too much money, spoiling her, depriving her, sending her to public school, sending her to private school, living in the city, being single, having lovers, not getting the film from her fifth birthday developed until she was six, and more.

I have heard the choir of discouragement. I have heard all the criticisms that come from relatives, friends, acquaintances and the world at large. And I have, at times, joined that choir. As one mother wrote in *Hip Mama* when she was describing all the "shoulds" she had heard since she bore her children, "When an outside critic wasn't on the case, I did the job myself." We have to stop that. Even when we cannot quiet our outside detractors, we have to resist the urge to join them.

One mom I know recently confessed that at three o'clock in the morning, after having tried to get her one-year-old to sleep for hours, she "lost it." She screamed, loud and fierce, "I am going to fucking die," and then leapt out of bed, ran to the front door of their studio apartment, and started kicking it. "I think I really frightened her," my friend kept telling me, as if her baby would be scarred for life. "I'll never forgive myself."

"Under the circumstances," I suggested, "'I am going to die' seems like a pretty reasonable thing to scream. And the door, well, a pretty reasonable thing to kick."

19

The world tells us all—in a thousand ways—that there is no margin of error in mothering. But I am here to tell you that there is a margin, and it is wide. Just as the occasional piece of chocolate cake can't make you fat, just as a few days off won't make you a lousy employee, blowing it as a mother every once in a while doesn't spell disaster for your kids' psyches. It simply doesn't.

We are human beings, after all, and sometimes we have to roar. We may feel caught between the tides, caught between who we are and who we think we ought to be, but we can also be honest. We can offer our children the whole of who we are, 3:00 A.M. roaring and all.

Take a moment to imagine the perfect mother. No, wait. Take a moment to look in the mirror. She is you. You are enough for your children, no matter what the choir says, no matter who you imagine you "should" be, you are enough. Remember that.

Pregnancy as B-Movie

I woke up on a damp morning in the summer of 1989, back cramped from sleeping six hours on the cobblestones of Rome's Campo dei Fiori, to my Siamese cat, Gitana, licking my nose. She had freed herself from the makeshift leash tied to my finger, but stayed close all night. I sat up slowly, and brushed off the back of my black leather jacket, a cheap biker necessity from Haight Street I had dragged across Europe.

In soft sunrise light, the market people were beginning to set up their stalls. Most of them passed the small heap of foreign riffraff, showing little more reaction than to twitch their noses or roll their eyes. We were not a novel sight: an American high school dropout and an Englishman three months out of jail roaming around the continent, money spent, arriving in Rome on a jumped train too late the night before to find a squat.

I took a deep breath of air filled with the smell of panini fresh out of an oven somewhere, stretched my arms in front of me, and tried not to vomit. I'd been pregnant for more than a month. I was getting good at keeping it down.

We had not come to Rome that July in search of ourselves or historical sights. We wouldn't visit the hill-town south of Naples my great-grandfather had left for a new life in America a century before. Instead, having just given up a two-month attempt to make some money on a potato farm in Spain, we had traveled along the shores of the Mediterranean to Rome on the advice of a homeless jewelry maker in Valencia. The Vatican hospital, he told us, offered free medical care to anyone who wandered in. It hadn't occurred to us that prenatal care would be useless if I couldn't communicate with my practitioner. But we had come this far, so after washing up in a tiny cafe bathroom and gulping down sweet cappuccinos, we were off. We would stop to visit an old acquaintance of my boyfriend's and then go see the Catholic doctor.

I don't remember why my boyfriend didn't end up at the hospital with me later that morning. We may have decided that bringing Gitana wouldn't be proper and left him cat-sitting on a street corner outside the thick Vatican walls. Or maybe he had strayed into a bar. I have managed to forget many of his antics during those months. He was sometimes thoughtful and sometimes violent but always unpredictable and confusingly well-intentioned. Our life together was not pure hell, but as I sat crouched in the dimly lit waiting room, barefoot and my bra already too tight, I knew that regardless of the fleeting nuclear fantasies that would cross my mind over the next eight months, I was going to be a single mom.

At nineteen I had unknowingly joined one of the groups of people Americans love to hate. I was one of the million American teenagers who get pregnant each year, about half of whom decide to have a baby. In answer to the nuns' first sign-languaged question, no, I didn't want an abortion. We would have gone to Paris for that.

I could trace my last period to May 1, just three weeks after a march for women's lives brought more than 250,000 people to Washington, D.C.—the largest protest rally since the August 1963 civil rights march on Washington. Adamantly pro-choice, I had marched for women's rights before, and would again, so to many friends and strangers it seemed odd that in the midst of a renewed struggle for reproductive freedom spurred by threats to the Supreme Court's 1973 decision in Roe v. Wade, I was ten thousand miles from home, looking for free services and using my reproductive freedom to decide to have a baby.

I was, after all, a classic candidate for an abortion. Although adult by military standards, I was a "child having a child" according to the rhetoric of the time. But for me abortion was an option rather than an obligation. I wanted to have a baby. And somewhere beneath my constant monologue of self-criticism and doubts about the future, I had a little faith and a well of confidence. I would be a good mother. The best.

I believed, as nineteen-year-olds in biker jackets roaming around Europe tend to, that life would always be all right, that nine months was ample time to conjure up a way to support myself and my child, and that if all else failed, God, or the Goddess, would provide.

As the solemn nun took my pulse and blood pressure that morning, I wasn't thinking about the future. All I wanted to know was that my baby was all right. After the once-over by the nun and a male doctor, they sighed with bewildered reassurance. I was fine. The baby would probably be fine. They didn't tell me what not to eat or drink. They didn't offer a follow-up appointment (they probably hoped I would be on the next plane back to the States). But their nods were enough for the time being.

Stepping out of the tiny office, I felt sick again, dizzy. I sat down on a soft gray-green chair. I must have looked pale, or terribly pathetic, because a moment later an elderly woman rushed in and knelt before me. She held my face in her hand, looked me right in the eye and wailed something in Italian. Tears welled up in her eyes. She crossed herself. I was speechless and disoriented and knew I simply could not puke on her. She vanished as quickly as she'd appeared.

Over the next eight months, I would take my own pulse at least a hundred times, imagining I could somehow gauge my health by it, but I remained calmly oblivious to what was going on in the country I had left behind to study in China and wander the globe more than three years earlier.

In 1989, the birth rate among U.S. teens was edging back up after slight declines between 1975 and 1986. Americans were in a panic. Politicians in many states had managed to cut Aid to Families with Dependent Children (AFDC) in hopes of curbing the number of births and gaining a few points in the polls, but most refused to acknowledge that their efforts did nothing to lower the birth rate among teenagers and may have even pushed the numbers up. The new frenzy over "skyrocketing" teenage pregnancy must have seemed curious to those who knew the actual statistics. Teen sex, pregnancy and motherhood were nothing new, nor was the slight rise in birth rates alarming in and of itself. What had changed, however, was that pregnant teens weren't getting married. Out-of-wedlock births had indeed "skyrocketed" since 1970, especially among European Americans, and there were no signs that the trend was fleeting. America was well on its way to becoming a nation of families headed by women, and that scared folks.

It was a mess I would walk into a year later, but one I couldn't have cared less about as we sat in a cheap restaurant that night, twirling spaghetti around forks and talking to a new friend who would soon offer us a giant key to her Tuscany apartment. I attributed my appetite for a second plate of pasta to "eating for two" and took the opportunity to crave gelato on an hourly basis.

We stayed with our new friend, Rita, on the outskirts of Rome for two nights. She was HIV-positive and pointed out dirty needles from IV drug use in the streets as she showed us *her* Rome—cafes, bars, piazzas. At the end of our stay, Rita sent us off with an iron key that looked as if it would open a castle and a hand-drawn map to the apartment that "needed work."

We hitchhiked for twenty-four hours to get to Sorano, a tiny hill-town surrounded by Etruscan caves. Another thirty minutes took us to the apartment near Elmo, a village that consisted of a bar and a post office. The Italian countryside around Sorano is much like parts of rural northern California where the population is an odd mix of disillusioned urban guitarists trying to get back to nature and middle-aged provincial couples whose children have long since moved to the city. The older people roll their eyes when they see strangers move in, and watch them closely for weeks before saying *Buon giorno*.

In any case, the living was cheap. Over the next few months, my boyfriend took odd jobs cleaning up olive orchards and restoring antique furniture. I worked sporadically and made cakes that sold for five dollars a slice at the summer arts fair. The days were long and hot, and as my *pancia* slowly ballooned and the blackberries that lined the roads grew sweeter, I would walk a few miles a day, singing Joan Armatrading songs to myself.

When I wasn't walking from place to place, I spent my time complaining that we had no running water or electricity, checking the post office for small parcels from home, shopping for vegetables and wine in town, and visiting Rosella, or one of the few other people in the area who spoke English or cared to listen to me fumble along in Italian. At night I cooked peppers, tomatoes and mushrooms with pasta. My boyfriend drank a liter of red wine, told stories of his boyhood in English boarding schools, dreamt of building a stone house nearby and shouted that the apartment was not clean enough, my cooking too spicy and my attitude disrespectful. As he slept I wrote long letters to my baby by candlelight. In the morning he would apologize, blaming his frustration on the wine. But what he said was true, and since I liked messes and spices, and had no intention of becoming a doormat, the breakup seemed more and more inevitable. My life was half fairy tale and half B-movie, but home seemed too far to travel now, and somewhere I held on to a belief in the fairy tale's and even the B-movie's happy ending. Everything might change when the baby was born.

Studies of teen parents show that many babies born to young women are wanted, but many of us are also ambivalent about our pregnancies and about motherhood. My own ambivalence was focused on the life I would build for my child. I wanted at once to be an American Super Mom and an Italian housewife; I wanted to buy a pink trailer near the California coast and a cafe in Sorano.

"You are living like an old Italian woman in the South who has no possibilities," Rosella once told me, leaning back against the wall of her house and looking out over the acres of olive trees she and her boyfriend rarely tended. "Not like an intelligent American woman who has been all over the world."

I was quiet and rubbed my eyes. "I don't have any energy. And it's so pretty here."

She laughed and shook her head. "I think you are lazy. I think you are too lazy to clean your house and too lazy to leave it," she said as she dragged on her cigarette.

By October I was visibly pregnant, and the dreamlike haze that surrounded me through two trimesters was fading. The days grew colder, strong winds hissed through the gap under our front door and the rains leaked through our roof and flooded the stone floor of our apartment that seemed more like a second-floor garage now. My boyfriend worked almost every day, I traveled about thirty miles to the hospital in Acqua Pendente for regular checkups and anchovy pizza, Gitana cried from our window for hours on end, and the neighbors, who now treated me with a mixture of amusement and concern, began to ask when we would be moving to a real home.

The "real home," it turned out, was a converted wine cellar next to the only pizzeria in Sorano. For one hundred dollars a month we had hot showers every day, a black-and-white TV, a couch bed and a portable stove. It seemed enough for the time being. But it was temporary. The owner lived in the house during the summer months, and because our lease would end then, or because we were growing tired of Italy or of each other, it seemed clear that by June, with infant child, together or separately, we would be on an airplane to somewhere else.

News of the San Francisco earthquake arrived via TV, and I waited by the pay phone in the piazza to get through to my parents. The Berlin Wall came down, and old veterans cried in the bars. Fall turned to winter, and I scrubbed the tile walls of the bathroom that mildewed daily because we had no shower curtain. My boyfriend lost his job and didn't find another. I walked less and danced more, and the doctor warned me that I still wasn't getting enough exercise.

The little house filled up with bags of tiny clothes and blankets, bottles and breast pumps, a buggy and a crib. I drank raspberry leaf tea and wrote poems in the morning that I burned at night. And at midnight on February 7, 1990, I looked at the travel clock next to our bed and knew I'd be a mother by morning.

The Fool

I'm a sucker for a good oracle. You won't catch me stall-hopping at the psychic fair, but if I want to know the right time to start work on a new book, I throw the I Ching. When I'm trying to figure out why a certain friend is so dreadfully mercurial, or why there seems to be so much exhaustion available to me on a given day, I check out the stars. When I need serious assistance—rent money, say, or inner peace—I go see the priestess in the barrio. She reads the shells and breaks it down for me, sending me off with a grocery list and a spell so precise I figure I could sue her if it didn't work. I don't have to. It works. Of course it works. And on the two occasions in my life when I was seriously considering having a kid—once ten years ago and once last week—I got out my dusty tarot cards and drew the Fool.

There he is—there he is again—skipping happy-go-lucky toward the cliff's edge. The only archetype who doesn't mind being laughed at. There he is—there he is again—trusting and tricking along like the Wile E. Coyote cartoon character. Obliviously fearless—he's got better things to do than survive.

So, here I am—here I am again. My rational, childless,

ever-miserable friends place hand on hip and use the other to
support a wagging index finger. You *know* better, they tell me.
And maybe I do. Surely there's a positive word for disaster.

Where the Dreams Go

*The dream, scrutinized by scientists in various experi-
ments, has been found to be an absolute necessity to
[wo]man. It keeps our psychic life alive, in its own proper
climate. It sustains life not corruptible and not suscep-
tible to the pressures of society. When we cease to believe
in this spiritual underground, to nourish ourselves on
feelings, our lives become empty shells, automatic,
mechanical.*

ANAÏS NIN, *The Novel of the Future*

In *Of Woman Born*, Adrienne Rich writes, "I remember thinking I would never dream again (the unconscious of the
young mother—where does it entrust its messages, when
dream-sleep is denied her for years?)."

A good question. I started asking around. I presented
thirty mamas with this quote, and their answers poured in.

What happens to us as chronically sleep-deprived new
mothers? Many of us feel as though we are going insane
(maybe we are). For many, the sleep deprivation causes
depression, impatience and chronic blah. But many also described a more complex—even oddly positive—experience of
sleeplessness.

SUSAN

I found my dream life intruded rudely into my so-called waking life. When I'm sleeping "normally," I go through typical cycles of dream REM sleep and non-dream sleep. But when I had an infant and was constantly being woken up, I would be in the midst of some really crazed dream, and I was always disoriented. The dream would kind of follow me around in my waking life and was much more intrusive than normal, and I wouldn't have the energy to push it back. My dreams were extremely vivid, bizarre and Technicolor during those sleep-broken nights, and then I'd have difficulty stuffing them back into my head, or wherever it was they came from. Now that we're all sleeping through the night, my dreams are thinner and more wispy, and I don't remember them as well, nor do they haunt me like they used to.

SERENA

At first it was maddening. I couldn't work. I couldn't function. I struggled with it. I drank coffee. I wanted to be the same person I was before the babies. But without sleep? How? Then something started to shift. Between the tiredness and the dreamlessness, I started to lose my defenses. I became softer. I became more honest. Because you cannot lie when you are that tired. My unconscious became my conscious, if that is possible. Nothing was repressed. Everything was expressed. I look at my journals from those early days, and I think, Wow, I had revelations in those first ten months that might have taken ten years in therapy to uncover.

At the risk of romanticizing torture, these descriptions point to the reality that early motherhood can also be an incredible opportunity for psychic development. All this interrupted sleep results in some merging of consciousness and unconsciousness. Boundaries fall away. We open up, we lay down our armor whether we want to or not. Because when we are this tired, we just can't bullshit ourselves or anyone else. For some of us, our dreams begin to follow us into waking life, filling it with surreal images. We become more open to our creative minds, and we learn, as Zora Neale Hurston wrote, "the dream is the truth."

If you find you have trouble remembering your night dreams and want to keep track of them, clean your room and turn your mattress over. Remake your bed with your favorite sheets. Put a lavender sachet under your pillow. Put fresh flowers—gerbera daisies are good—in a vase on your nightstand. Eat a light dinner, and pass on the wine. Before you go to sleep tie a midnight-blue ribbon around your wrist and announce clearly to yourself that you are going to remember whatever you dream. Have your journal and a pen ready so that you can write down your dreams as soon as you wake up. Often dream memories last only a few minutes after we wake up. You have to catch them while you can.

Seven Pregnant Dreams

I.   A Chinese woman is riding her bicycle toward me. She has two chickens in a basket on the back. She honks her little horn at me as I cross the street. "Get out of the way, White Ghost Girl," she shouts in Chinese.

II.   I am in a squat in London. I go downstairs because I hear some commotion. I open the door to the neighbor's apartment, and the woman who lives there is holding up her husband's still-pulsing heart. "Do you guys have central heating?" I ask.

III.   I am swimming in the South China Sea. The water turns turquoise, then white, then orange. I become a fish and swim to the bottom, where I find a small ruby ring. As I pick it up, it turns into a snake. I notice I have borne a baby in the water.

IV.   A Chinese woman is riding her bicycle down the street. She has a swan in a basket on the back. "Slow down, White Ghost Girl," she says as she passes. "You're in a different time zone now."

V.   I am in a squat in Rome. I wake up because a woman is screaming at my boyfriend. "What does she want?" I mumble. The woman goes silent, comes to the bed, lifts me up, and together we float out the tiny window and over the darkened city.

VI.   I am driving around San Francisco looking for a hospital where I can have the baby, but they are all closed or under construction. I give birth in the car—to an eight-pound piglet. I wake up feeling guilty because I had so wanted a human baby.

VII.   I am sitting in a movie theater next to a ten-year-old girl with long, dark hair. The credits are rolling. I lean over and whisper, "I don't know your name yet." She whispers, "Maia."

Children Need Interesting Mothers

Lately I've noticed a particularly disturbing classified ad popping up in various publications. It goes something like this: "Every Mother's Dream: Stay Home, Lose Weight. For more information, call 1-800 . . . " The ad is annoying on many levels, but let's focus on the worst. Imagine for a moment this ad said: "Every Father's Dream: Stay Home, Lose Weight" or "Every Child's Dream: Stay Home, Lose Weight." The ad just wouldn't fly. Dads and kids aren't supposed to "Stay Home, Lose Weight." They're supposed to be well taken care of, and then they are supposed to go out and lead adventurous lives.

But mothers are a different species, right? We're supposed to be whittling ourselves away in our apartments wanting nothing more than to be as small as possible while serving our kin fabulous lasagna, right? I don't think so. As mothers, we are encouraged to give and give and give, and at the end of the day, when we have given all we have, we are encouraged to go on diets, carefully measuring anything we might dream of giving ourselves.

"Children need interesting mothers," the feminist scholar Marge Frantz once noted. And mothers need interesting lives. We don't need to "Stay Home, Lose Weight," although we may, on occasion, want to do one or both of those things. More often we need to sleep. We need time to ourselves, moments of awareness, connections, meaningful work. We need cheap art, good sex, nights at the bowling alley and days at the beach. We need good coffee, hearty meals, lush gardens and time to relax and enjoy our lives without worrying so much about whether we are good enough mothers or skinny enough girlfriends or wives. We need to take care of ourselves so that we can mother our children soulfully and lead lives worth living.

If you are still afraid that only a "selfless" mother can do right by her children, maybe you'll just have to take my word for it. As the diarist Anaïs Nin said, "We will always have a conflict between our growth and our fear that that growth will overshadow or injure someone else." Namely, our kids. But remember, when we talk about taking care of ourselves, we are not talking about neglecting our children. We are talking about practicing and modeling self-respect, self-care and self-empowerment. As Mati, a hipmama.com community member, wrote, "If I were not following some of my own dreams and hopes, a spark would be missing from within myself that might have helped ignite sparks in my daughter's life."

It's not always easy to take time for ourselves, but it is doable. No matter how rich or broke we are, and no matter how many husbands, lovers and children we've got vying for our attention, it's doable, and it's vital.

Bargaining with the Patriarchy

The history of motherhood in America is the history of economics, war, Judeo-Christian and Puritan morality and, finally, feminism. In the colonies, fathers were usually the primary caregivers for children. Work and family life were fully integrated then, but three hundred years of witch hunts left us without our midwives and terrified the survivors. Many women died in childbirth, but even living mamas were considered too "impure" to raise their own kids.

Fast-forward to the Revolutionary War. The men were needed in the battlefields to fight Great Britain (an enemy who was portrayed in propaganda posters as an evil mother-whore!). Child-care responsibilities started shifting to Mom—but with a few strings attached.

In the new nation, ideas of "republican motherhood" were all the rage. With some self-improvement work, it seemed we women could overcome our evil natures and inhabit a pedestal of female purity from which we could be trusted with the moral upbringing of our kids. Believe it or not, this backwards evolution from whore to virgin status was progress. Or at least it was a way to stay alive.

Enter the Victorian era, "the cult of true womanhood" and

the concept that women should be responsible for the "separate sphere" of the home. Throw in the Industrial Revolution and the Civil War—when the guys left home again to fight or work in the factories—and here's where the whole breadwinner father/stay-at-home mother/isolated nuclear family prototype got started, just a half-dozen generations ago.

Of course, poor women and people of color in this country have always worked outside their own homes, caring for other people's children and doing underpaid labor in the factories and the fields. And America has always had her eccentrics, her artists, her rebels and her feminists. So the whole housewife/factory-husband/nuclear family thing was then, as it is now, more often the ideal than the reality.

To reinforce that ideal and our womanly place in it, the Presbyterian church gave women *Mother's Magazine* in 1833. That was followed by A. J. Graves's popular tome of the 1840s, *Woman in America*. Here we learned that a woman could "operate far more efficiently in promoting the great interests of humanity by supervising her own household than in any other way."

Thank you, A. J.

And in case we were thinking about slacking off on our laundry duties, in 1883 and 1885 respectively, *Ladies' Home Journal* and *Good Housekeeping* hit the stands. As Frances Willard, president of the conservative National Woman's Christian Temperance Union from 1879 to 1898 put it, "womanliness first, afterwards what you will."

So here was the patriarchal bargain: our freedom in exchange for protection and security. Over the first sixty years of the twentieth century, millions of us would make the trade.

Wars and economic changes challenged our new family "traditions" in the early 1900s, but again and again, scientific propaganda came to the rescue, producing all kinds of "proof" that conveniently confirmed a woman's place. The study of psychology and child-development ensued, but for every helpful discovery we got another piece of thinly veiled misogyny designed to keep us busy and make us feel guilty.

When "science" wasn't enough to keep us in line, the government stepped in with cash incentives. The most dramatic example of this happened in the late 1940s and 1950s. During World War II, women were in the paid labor force in unprecedented numbers. After the war, until 1947, divorce rates surged, but with a little help from the mass media and those handy little government-subsidized house-ownership plans, Rosie the Riveter went home and the industrial/nuclear family model came back with a vengeance. Some mamas made a break for it, but after two world wars, a depression and a holocaust, you can hardly blame the ones who were ready to pop some prescription drugs and give up just about anything for home ownership on a single income—a little stability.

But a funny thing happened. The Valium wore off. TVs in every home started filling our heads with images—and possibilities. The civil rights movement, the renaissance of the 1960s, the antiwar movement and the feminist, environmental and consciousness movements sprung into action. Throw in the end of the industrial age, and the nuclear family was on a fast track to extinction. By the time I was born in 1970, life was all about choices, options, movements.

For a brief time, it looked as if we might be able to re-invent family in a single generation. As a kid, I considered my freedoms to be self-evident: Choices were my birthright. Would I marry, or would I stay single? Would I go to college, or would I drop out of high school to hitchhike around the world? Would I have kids? Would I stay home, or would I work for pay? Would I be queer or straight? Would I move to an ashram, or would I live in the world?

What I didn't realize until my adult life was upon me was that all those choices had become obsolete. I would live an overwhelming "all of the above." But something else happened, too.

After more than a hundred years of being forced to depend on a husband's paycheck for our survival, and just a decade after we might have revolutionized all of that, we got a backlash against feminism. We got Dan Quayle tripping out about Murphy Brown. We got a full-fledged crusade designed to high-tail it back to the nineteenth century before we got to the twenty-first. At the same time, the living-wage jobs were shipped off to sweatshops in the developing world, mass quantities of drugs continued to be dumped into our communities, and record numbers of our young men were arrested and imprisoned on charges directly related to poverty and those drugs.

In the 1930s, our economic troubles were met with a "New Deal." But in 1995, we got propaganda that depicted single moms as the new evil whores and, adding insult to injury, we got the "Personal Responsibility Act."

Thank you, Newt.

But at least the boys in D.C. were finally being honest about the value of all those bargains we'd made with the patriarchy. Junk bonds.

Still, freedom is the bright side of nothing left to lose.

The days of either/or are all but over now. We will all work, and we will all be at home. Many of us will experience times of support and times of isolation. We will have mystical revelations while we're doing the dishes. We will learn lessons in classrooms and on the road. Theoretically, we have more choices than ever. But without the economic power to pursue our true choices, we are left running in circles between desire and necessity, dancing optimistically toward the future, but trying to make our lives work here and now, in the middle of this incomplete revolution.

Learning to Be Unacceptable

"Learning to Be Unacceptable." That was the headline that gave me my first real understanding that there were things mothers did not do. The story underneath the headline told of a divorced mother and the Roman Catholic priest she was about to marry.

I was five years old.

Palo Alto was a small town then—or I was small enough to experience it as one. A small town made smaller by the fact that the divorced mother was my own and the Roman Catholic priest, my soon-to-be stepfather. Some journalists had more fun with the story: It's hard not to love a headline like "Man of God Torn from Cloth by Temptress Named Eve!" even if that temptress is your mother.

And understand, my mother didn't have to *learn* to be unacceptable. As a single gal with kids, as a welfare mom living in a converted garage, as a feminist and a sexual being, well—in the order of maternal dos and don'ts, my mother's engagement to the priest was hardly her first offense. But it was the first one I was conscious of.

In the early months of my parents' romance, my sister and I learned to make a game of their secret. John—"Father

Duryea"—was sick for a time, and my mom wore a Smoky the Bear mask when we visited him in the hospital. As he recovered on the pull-out sofa-bed in our living room, blue-haired ladies rang our doorbell snooping after rumors. My sister and I would stall them in the entryway as my mom hurried John into a closet. Then my mom would make small talk with the ladies as my sister and I hid eyeglasses, slippers and all the rest of the evidence of the priest's unacceptable presence in our lives.

It wasn't until our family secret was out that I understood why we'd kept it at all.

Of course, Roman Catholic priests have their own set of dos and don'ts. They *preach* of love. They do not *fall* in love. John refused to declare that his priesthood had been a mistake from the start—a gesture that might have garnered him the equivalent of an annulment from his post. Instead, he told the bishop the truth and was swiftly excommunicated. He would have been expelled from the church no matter who he'd chosen as his bride. But in that small town that seemed to me to be growing smaller every day, the crux of the scandal was the particular woman he had fallen for: the divorced mother, the woman named Eve.

All but a few of the faithful among the large community John had served in his thirty-some years as a priest—those he had baptized, married, harbored from the draft and forgiven many times over—turned their backs on him, and behind my mother's back in the local co-op, they whispered "witch."

There were things mothers did and things they did not do, after all. The journalists knew it. The bishop knew it. The church community knew it. The co-op shoppers knew it. And now I knew it, too.

Mothers did not live without men. They did not lead lives of their own. And they did not marry the local Catholic priest. Simple.

Those were the first maternal rules I learned. Over the years I'd learn many more and, like the first three, only after they'd been broken. But I learned to be unacceptable young.

That June I wore a Guatemalan dress and carried daises down the aisle of Memorial Church for my parents' wedding. My mother laughed. John blushed. A group of friends pitched in and bought them a dishwasher.

After the ceremony, my mother sent the journalists away. We had no further comment, she told them. We already knew how to be unacceptable, thank you.

We moved into John's childhood home. I hiked up and down the hallway for hours, counting every lap as a mile. And relieved of the burden of upholding a respectable reputation, we all settled into that summer and into our unacceptable new lives.

Self-Centered

This morning's paper shouts a boldface headline: "Parents Fail." The gist of the story is that parents today, mothers in particular, are a bunch of self-centered brats. And our children are paying the price for our selfishness.

A woman on the sidewalk below my balcony screams at her son to get in the car "or else."

A friend is on the phone asking if I'll watch her two kids—ages two years and six months—for the weekend. I tell her I can't. Anyway, they are still nursing. How could I? Then I realize it's an emergency. My friend hasn't had a moment to herself in nearly a year and she feels as if she's about to go the way of the other headline this morning, "Mother Strangles Infant." I offer to take them for the day.

The woman across the street has, apparently, been locked out of the house and is yelling at her daughter to "open the door, open the door, open the door!" Finally she threatens, "I'm gonna whip you when I get in there." (I wouldn't open the door either if I were the kid.)

The woman feigning patience in the back yard next to mine takes care of seven kids nine hours a day for a living. The kids are happy enough. They don't seem to notice that the only difference between their caregiver and the one across the street is that this one is keeping her frustration to herself.

My dictionary defines "self-centered" as "caring for yourself at the expense of others." But I know something the newspaper and the dictionary do not. I know the insanity of this hour has more to do with not being centered at all. Not being centered on the self. Not being in tune with what we need long before the panicked phone calls to friends, long before the hurtful words jump from our lips, long before we have to dream up what "or else" might mean.

Maybe I should have offered to take my friend's kids for two hours a week last year when I could see she was going to drive herself crazy nursing those two babies, letting them sleep in her bed, never taking time to center on herself. But I didn't think of it. Maybe she should have asked me.

When I go out back to get my laundry off the clothesline, I ask the woman baby-sitting the seven kids how she's doing. "I'm about to lose my last marble," she says with a bright, bogus smile.

"You need a break, girl," I tell her.

And she nods. "I know." She picks up her cordless phone and plans a mini-vacation for the weekend after this one. When she puts the phone down, she exhales. "Just knowing I'm going away makes this all doable."

The soul knows what it needs. Sometimes we need a reminder to listen, but it always knows. Trouble is, instead of reminders to take care of ourselves, we get called names in the newspaper. We do our best, we do better than our best, we push ourselves and push ourselves, and then we collapse.

On hipmama.com, the mothers call it "the edge of Mommy," and they know it's coming when, as Jess Marie Walker described in a post,

You can't or won't slow down—when you can barely breathe. When you can rationalize anything and everything you do, regardless. When your tolerance levels are low and tantrums are often. When you can't get out of bed after a perfectly good night's sleep. When you refuse fresh air, healthy food and water. When you can't think clearly, remember anything, keep up with it all even after you wrote the list five times. When you can't stop crying and you have worn everybody out and then you can't stop laughing and you have worn everybody out. When you think you are too weak and when you think you are so strong you can contain every molecule in your sweet little mind without realizing that combustion is on its way in a minute and if you don't allow someone with experience to carry some of the weight there could be an explosion. And then where will their mother be?

She'll be out on the sidewalk screaming with the rest of them. She'll be on the phone. She'll be in the newspaper. "Your children need you healthy and clear," Jess reminds. *You* need you healthy and clear.

It Takes a Heap of Loafing to Raise a Kid

When Maia was a baby and we lived in the suburbs, I was the envy of my neighborhood. It was a neighborhood of mostly white, middle-class two-parent families with jobs and cars and annual vacations and forty-thousand-plus incomes. But the moms on my block envied me, the poor single student mom with the big natty hair and the noisy old car. It took me a long time to figure out what it was about my life that intrigued them and why they lingered so long in my doorway, asking to hide scribbled poems in my cupboard and confiding their wildest dreams of lives that sounded oddly similar to my own.

It didn't hit me until several years later when I asked the readers of *Hip Mama* to think about motherhood's greatest taboos—our most secret thoughts and wishes. To my initial surprise, the majority of the responses reminded me of my old suburban friends' yearnings. Our taboos didn't have to do with sex or food or any of those traditional female "sins." What we wanted was simple: an hour alone. Different readers expressed their wishes in different ways. Some dreamed of taking a bath without having to listen for the toddler.

49

Some imagined sleeping a whole night through. And one boldly posted a message on hipmama.com: "Give me joint custody, hold the divorce!" Once this married mom confided this universal desire to the online community, dozens more chimed in with their own hopes or rituals for an hour to themselves or a mellow afternoon without any schedules or "to do" lists.

What my suburban neighbors had envied was not my big hair, or my crappy car, or my five-hundred-dollar-a-month income, or even my singleness. They just wanted to spend a day in their pajamas every once in a while, as I did. I was hardly a woman of leisure, but in our picture-perfect suburban neighborhood, I was the next best thing. My neighbors envied my ability to slack. They envied my ability to say, *Hey, the baby is whining and I've got three papers due tomorrow and I'm in the middle of an ugly family-court battle and I can't pay my rent tomorrow, but you know what? I'm going to take a bath.* I believed in and practiced attachment parenting, but I also knew that I was not the Energizer bunny.

As a young single mom, I had a head start breaking free of the cultural expectations of motherhood. "That's what I like about you," my neighbor Paula told me as I was hanging some whack homemade Christmas decorations. "You don't care what anybody thinks."

Paula imagined that I was personally evolved, but not caring what anybody thought was, at first, sour grapes. And I learned to loaf not because I knew it was important, but because I simply couldn't keep going and going and going.

My friend Wendy calls me a closet overachiever posing as a slacker, but I've learned that there's a connection.

When I was working on my first book, I sometimes felt the project required more discipline than I had in me. I spent too many of the hours I was supposed to be writing chapters lying on the couch eating seasoned curly fries or painting my toenails blue. I'd spend two hours slacking, two hours stressing out and feeling guilty about having slacked, and about an hour writing.

Then one day as I lay on my couch reading—in slacker mode—I came across a beautiful little Gertrude Stein quote, and I stuck it on the wall right next to my couch: "It takes a heap of loafing to write a book."

I took her words like gospel and I loafed, cut out the two hours feeling guilty about it, wrote, and finished my book two months ahead of schedule. Now I've made another little sign that seems to me even more important: "It takes a heap of loafing to raise a kid." If Gertrude Stein had had children, I'm sure she'd have said it herself.

We are taught that motherhood is a selfless profession, but I'm here to tell you that it doesn't have to be. We can loaf. We can meet our children's needs and fulfill our own desires. We can take care of ourselves—not just because our own comfort and happiness will make us better parents (although it will)—but because we deserve the same attention we give to our kids. We are worth the trouble.

Education of a Mother

In the late 1970s, American divorce rates were maxed out, while the popularity of marriage was at an all-time low. Multiracial families were becoming so prevalent in the Bay Area, and "melting-pot" theories so commonplace, my friends and I all figured we'd meld into a lovely coffee brown by the turn of the millennium.

Of course, there would be a backlash. Change doesn't take much time. It's the backlashes that get you checking your watch. But we didn't know that at the time. We were in grade school. We were accustomed to growth spurts and disappearing relatives and irrevocable transformations that happened overnight. And we assumed the mandatory nuclear families of TV reruns and our mothers' childhood memories were a thing of the past. The Olden Days.

My first hard-core best friend showed up in the second grade. Her name was Stephie Chin, and my compassion was piqued when our teacher had her instruct the whole class on how to count in Chinese (*yī-èr-sān-sì!*). I don't know how I knew, but I knew for certain that Stephie would have preferred to hang upside-down off the edge of the Golden Gate Bridge than to teach our second grade class how to do anything in Chinese. Still, she did it. And because I, too, was easily mortified and inexplicably compliant, we were fast friends.

Every day after school we'd pick up Stephie's little brother and the three of us would walk halfway across town to their run-down two-story house. We spent the afternoon there, ostensibly in the care of Stephie's ā-pó, an ancient woman who lived in the house and barked a combination of Chinese and English gleaned from Tom and Jerry cartoons, and who basically didn't give a rat's ass what we did with our time.

What the three of us did was a fair amount of shoplifting. We also blew things up in the vacant lot next to their house with fireworks from ā-pó's basement and CO_2 cartridges from the local hardware store.

At sundown we'd scrub ourselves clean and then greet Stephie's mom with innocent smiles as she came up the back stairs carrying little plastic baggies of groceries that she'd turn into the most sublime meals I had ever tasted. We ate chicken drumettes and vegetables over rice, and I fell quietly in love with the whole family.

Stephie's mom had brought the kids to America "for a better life" a few years before and worked long hours at a local hospital. Stephie's father was dead. Her first memory, Stephie told me, was his funeral. All that was left of him was a strange colorized portrait that had been photo-transferred onto a plate that looked as if it had been broken and super-glued together many times over. It stood propped up now next to the night-light in the bedroom.

Ā-pó inhabited the ground floor of the house, and Stephie, her brother and their mother shared a single room upstairs. I remember our sleep-overs and how I envied the way the whole family slept together—with that strange colorized father-plate illuminated on the nightstand.

My best friend from fifth grade was Rosa. She lived in a house behind a house behind a house with her mother, Mary, her teenage sister and her sister's two-year-old son. Mary went to school full-time and worked two or three jobs to support the lot of them. Rosa was shy, a year younger than I was, but she already wore mascara and eyeliner. As I waited for her mom to pick me up for our first play date, I envisioned a large, elegant Latina woman with Princess Leia braids. Instead, a slim white mama who walked with a limp appeared at our door. Rosa's sister, whom Rosa and I both worshipped, was gorgeous and gregarious. Her son—born when she was fourteen or fifteen—was sweet, with big brown eyes that could melt the most exhausted heart.

Why I latched on to this family so immediately, I do not know, except that there was an intrinsic unacceptability about them and a matrilineal sensibility that didn't have to be named. They didn't know anything about "tough love," the disciplinary fad of the moment. The girls knew that no matter what happened, if they ran away, if they started doing drugs, if they got themselves knocked up, no matter what, when they were good and ready to come home, someone would open the door for them. Maybe this sounds natural. But Palo Alto, by the time I met Rosa, was Silicon Valley. The families were getting richer. And the money seemed to bring with it an arrogance and a "we don't need each other" kind of attitude.

When Rosa finished elementary school, she and Mary moved to Southeast Asia. Rosa's sister and her son followed.

My mom had finished grad school and was a human rights worker as well as an artist by then, and my stepdad worked at a bookstore and said Mass to his new alterna-Catholic community on Sundays. He cooked, she cleaned, he stressed about money, she stressed about time, and one of them was always home.

By the time I graduated from the misery of middle school and was trying to convince myself I could survive four years of high school, I knew about as many kids who lived with both parents as I knew Republicans, which is to say that although I'm sure they existed—judging by the fact that Ronald Reagan was still in office—our paths hardly ever crossed. Nora's dad was gay and lived with his partner in South Carolina. Sid's dad had recently left, and good riddance as far as I could tell. Amy lived every other week at her dad's, and Jennifer spent weekends on her dad's farm up north. Lilly's dad had never been there to begin with. Nor Steve's. Nor Holly's. Shakira's dad was rumored to be a political prisoner somewhere far away. Stephie's father was still dead, as was Mimi's. Aaron's father lived in Canada with a new wife and kid. Ella's father, Bill's father, Shelle's father— all were too long gone to be worth asking after. There was one father who lived near the high school, but I assume that he, too, would have left had he not shot his wife in the chest at point-blank range. Several of my neighbors had fathers at home, but I didn't know them. Guy, my first real boyfriend, confessed to me on our first quasi-date that he lived with both of his biological parents. Always had. His dad was a black civil rights activist turned professor and his mom was a white Jewish librarian who was kind and quiet. In 1985, in that once-small town, Guy and I, although nontraditional by some standards, came from the closest approximations of traditional nuclear families as anybody we knew.

Most of the mothers had day jobs, many had advanced degrees, some had remarried, others hoped to. And though we had no shortage of complaints about our mothers, they worked their asses off, and we knew it. We wanted our moms to have their educations, their equal rights and pay—but we also secretly longed for those fabled breadwinner fathers who were said to have provided for their families once upon a long ago time.

My bio-dad has been hard for me to know. As a kid, I saw him about once a year. We didn't reconnect until I was in college. Sort of an existentialist malfunction, he has the habit of disagreeing—across the board—with even my most mundane assumptions about reality. The kind of guy, to start quoting Bertrand Russell, who wouldn't admit it was certain that there wasn't a rhinoceros in the room. But he is also goodhearted. And I'm glad to know him.

My stepdad is kind and constant. My mom, for her part, is all Scorpio—all passion. I can't imagine what our house would have been like without John, who served as a kind of surge protector. Still, my mom was the center of our family. No questions. Just as my friends' moms were the center of theirs. I am who I am because of my mother. If I have a backbone, it's because my mother saw to it that I developed one. And when it has failed me, she has never hesitated to kick ass on my behalf.

Don't Adjust

The absurdity of our culture's contradictory expectations of mothers was painfully illustrated for me last year when I was in the middle of a family-court battle that led me into a labyrinth of "help" services peopled by social workers, judges, lawyers, psychiatrists and "experts" of every kind. Although each of these professionals was supposed to help my family, their job, it turned out, was more to "evaluate" than to assist.

How would they evaluate my family? How would they evaluate me? I didn't give this much thought at first. I figured I was like most people: a human being made of shadows and light. I figured I was a confident, "good enough" mother, a mother who gave child-rearing much thought. I figured anyone could see these things. But I figured wrong.

Sure, I am like most people. But these professionals were not there to empathize with my universal dilemmas. They were on duty to uphold and enforce all those conflicting cultural expectations.

By the time the professionals were done "evaluating" me, every decision I had ever made as a mom—including my decision to become one—had been scrutinized, put on trial and, ultimately, found lacking. When the dust finally settled,

I had been called too young, too serious, too quiet, too aggressive, overinvolved, neglectful, hypervigilant, oblivious, promiscuous, prudish, hysterical and remote. Along the way I had been advised to "speak up," to "shut up," to "let go" and to "never let go." I was asked by one professional why I hadn't had an abortion and prodded by another, "I understand you were once married to a woman." I was characterized by a social worker as overly soft, and by a psychiatrist as an ice queen with a vendetta. I was faulted as a mother for working too much and, at the same time, billed more than twenty thousand dollars for the insults.

When I frightened these professionals with the truth, they called me angry. When that made me angry, they nodded and recommended therapy. When I went to therapy, I was diagnosed as suffering from an "adjustment disorder with mixed disturbance of emotions." Translation: failure to adjust to a deranged world.

I bit my lip and asked the therapist, "But if I adjust, won't you say I'm totally dysfunctional?"

She nodded.

When I asked for an alternative remedy, she threw up her arms and laughed, "Revolution? Gardening?"

Family-court battle or no, I know a lot of folks who are suffering from adjustment disorders with mixed disturbance of emotions. As far as these professionals—and the greater culture their opinions reflect—are concerned, we mothers are all damned if we do, crazy if we don't. We are handed a tangle of conflicting expectations and faulted for having conflicting responses to those expectations.

God knows what would have become of me if I had entered

into the whole process underconfident or accused of any actual wrongdoing. As it was, my year with the professionals stripped me of most of my confidence and some of my kindness, too.

In the end I "won," meaning my original wishes became my reality.

I walked home slowly then, padded up the stairs into my apartment, read my daughter a strange bedtime story filled with fairies and ripening fruit and sang her to sleep. In the dark, I burned those contradictory reports and told myself I wasn't *too*-anything.

I slept soundly and rose with the sun to do some potted plant gardening and some thinking. And while I rested on my blue patio chair, contemplating the fresh dirt under my nails, I decided that those professionals—who never agreed with one another—were all right. I am too-everything. And I wouldn't have it any other way.

Now give me a catch-22 of motherhood, and I will swallow it whole: I stay at home, and I work for pay. I am modest, and I flaunt it. I subscribe to *People* and to *Ms.* I am single, and I am in love. I do dishes constantly, and my sink is full. I am wildly ambitious, and I loaf for hours on end. I am the best mother any child could hope to have, and I am the worst. I am good at making money and even better at wasting it. I am clear-headed, and I am completely insane. I am a Cancer, Aries moon, shy and fierce (just thought I'd warn you). I am angry, but I am right.

I learned a good deal from those professionals (although, perhaps, none of what they meant to teach me). I learned that small miracles come after a lot of hard work and a good fight (revolutions are made of a hundred thousand small miracles). I learned that two professionals on a case are usually worse than none. Three can be dangerous. And I learned that to live well and mother soulfully amid all of the contradictions, we don't have to adjust to anything. The remedy is distilled from equal parts gardening and revolution.

System Error

When the phone is ringing, and the infant is fussing, and the toddler is whining about a Luke Skywalker action figure, and the seven-year-old can't find his shoes and is about to miss the school bus, and you turn on the computer and a little picture of a bomb appears with a message that reads, "Sorry, a system error has occurred," and the kettle is whistling, and the cat is hungry, and there is spitup on your briefcase (the dark-brown leather one that appeared last Christmas and that you never wrote a thank-you note for but now it's too late because you can't remember who sent it), and you have to pee, and your lover is hogging the bathroom, and you get an e-mail message from a friend who is convinced that "the end is nigh," and you remember suddenly that your mother is coming for dinner and you had promised to make the chicken mole from the Frida Kahlo cookbook and you can't even begin to imagine where the cookbook is, and the infant is still fussing, and you step on the Luke Skywalker action figure and sprain your ankle, it's all right not to get frantic. Take a seat. Take a breath. And let yourself laugh. This is how it is meant to be sometimes.

Children Are Not Pizza Pies

In a recent midnight conversation with my mother, we spoke of various problems in my own life and in my sister's. As it got later my mother started asking, "Where did I go wrong?" Setting aside the reality that I was a wee bit insulted by her question, I had to remind her that regardless of our problems this was not a useful question.

As far as I'm concerned, there are only about three things we have to do for our kids: Nurture them in a child-friendly culture or subculture; give them appropriate limits and boundaries; and refuse to abandon them. Will following these three rules guarantee you ever-happy, problem-free children? No. There is no such thing as an ever-happy, problem-free person. If there were, she would probably die of boredom.

We put everything we have into our kids, but they do not turn out predictably. They do not "turn out" at all. They are human, always changing. We can't parent them in a totally controlled environment. When things go wrong in their lives, we can rarely pinpoint a precise cause and effect, like "Holy shit, I used salt instead of sugar!" or "I shouldn't have kneaded so hard!"

If you are feeling hopelessly out of control, torturing yourself and your children asking where you went wrong, if you feel as if you need to undertake something with a predictable outcome, one that will turn out or not turn out based on the sum of the ingredients you put in, based on your timing, and on precise temperatures, try making a pizza pie:

In a small bowl, dissolve one package active dry yeast with a pinch of sugar in a half-cup of one-hundred-degree water. Let it stand for five to ten minutes. In a bigger bowl, combine two cups all-purpose flour and a teaspoon of salt. Add two tablespoons of olive oil and the yeast mixture. Blend well. Now add a pinch of rosemary and a quarter-cup of warm water, and mix some more. Dump the dough onto a floured board and knead for about ten minutes. Place the dough in an oiled bowl, cover it with a warm, damp cloth, and let it rise for up to two hours, or until it has doubled in bulk.

While you're waiting, make some tomato sauce. First sauté half an onion, minced, and a clove of garlic, minced, in about three tablespoons of olive oil for five minutes. Now stir in a pound of cored and chopped ripe tomatoes, or a twenty-eight-ounce can of peeled whole tomatoes. Add a pinch each of sugar, salt and pepper. Simmer, stirring occasionally, for about half an hour. Purée the mixture and simmer for another fifteen minutes.

After the dough has risen, punch it down. Oil a fourteen-inch pizza pan, and sprinkle it with a little cornmeal. Now roll out the dough into a quarter-inch-thick round, fling it up in the air a few times like they do on TV, and lay it out onto your pizza pan, pinching it up around the edges. Brush the dough with olive oil, and preheat your oven to 425 degrees.

Now spread the dough with your tomato sauce, leaving a one-inch border, and cover it with thin slices of mozzarella cheese and about two tablespoons of grated parmesan. The rest of the toppings are up to you. Arrange as you see fit: anchovies, pepperoni, salami, shrimp, chopped garlic, black olives, artichoke hearts, thinly sliced onions, green peppers, chopped mushrooms, zucchini or whatever you like.

Pour yourself a glass of red wine, and spend about ten minutes contemplating how marvelously boring life would be if you only had simple, albeit time-consuming, recipes for every endeavor you undertook.

Now bake your pizza pie for twenty to twenty-five minutes in the lower third of the oven.

PART II

Beware of those who talk about sacrifice

I think there is choice possible at any moment to us, as long as we live. But there is no sacrifice. There is a choice, and the rest falls away. Second choice does not exist. Beware of those who talk about sacrifice.

MURIEL RUKEYSER, *The Life of Poetry*

Circus Acts

I want to get something clear: Juggling is for circus clowns.

When Maia and I moved back to California from Italy, I did what I thought I ought to: I tried on the cultural myth of the time. I tried to become a Super Mom, "juggling" the various elements of my life: family, work, school, art, friends, love, sex, politics and personal time. I sought to "balance" all of these elements. I bought a day planner and imagined that if I wrote everything down, compartmentalizing my life into fifteen-minute segments, I might master the impossible. Around the same time, I started trying to balance my checkbook, imagining that if I could only add and subtract correctly, I'd have enough money. Both schemes improved my math skills. Neither made the days longer or my bank account fuller. The time and money constraints I faced were real, but they were also hopelessly intertwined with the cultural myths that cluttered my mind. I wanted to believe that there was a solution in which I could have enough time and enough money while simultaneously giving myself entirely to my daughter, to my work, to my professors, to political movements, to my friends, to my lovers and to myself. And

I hoped to achieve all this with the appearance of effortlessness. No one had yet told me, as my friend the poet and novelist Opal Palmer Adisa finally did, that "being a good mother is too many jobs for one person."

In her book, *The Mother Dance,* author and psychologist Harriet Lerner says that women often come into therapy presenting their struggles with time, money and "perfect mother" expectations as if our predicament were some kind of neurotic disorder that might be cured with "the acquisition of new skills and a brighter attitude."

But we all soon discover that there are no new skills to acquire. The neurotic feeling comes from packing so much into our daily "to do" lists that we leave no time for reflection, strolling, conversation and storytelling. We forgo the spaces between activities, imagining we can cut corners this way. But, of course, the soul requires those spaces between events and tasks. Our emotional well-being depends on time for reflection. We have only one body, only twenty-four hours in each day. And often, we feel like "something's gotta give." Don't let it be the seemingly empty spaces.

The other day I was driving an acquaintance home from a school play our daughters had been in. An old Indigo Girls tape was playing on my car stereo. The mother seemed a little uneasy, but I imagined it was because my car was so messy, or because the girls were squealing relentlessly in the back seat. When the lyric "how I wish I were a trinity . . . "

played, the mother finally confessed: "This was my colic tape."

I understood. Her daughter is eight now, but we do not soon forget those long, strange nights spent comforting the baby and pacing. Nor that odd wish to have three of ourselves. One could sleep, one could continue life as we once knew it, and one could remain, with the baby, comforting, pacing, lost in the surreal half-sleep of early motherhood.

To call our experiences "juggling" is laughable. It belittles the work we do. Perhaps we'll achieve the awkward grace of circus clowns at some point in our motherhood, yes. Perhaps we'll feel compartmentalized for a time, too, or like trinities. But ultimately each of us has to reinvent the art of living, integrating all the old and new aspects of ourselves into a whole.

"When I say in my song that I was born with three dollars and six dimes," I heard the mother and R&B diva Erykah Badu explain between sets at a show recently, "what I mean to say is that I was born whole. I was not broke."

The task isn't to master the clown's art of juggling the broken pieces. The task is to remain whole. And it's in the empty spaces that we catch glimpses of our whole selves, where we have time to fit the pieces together.

You Can Have It All, but Do You Want It?

Work is a four-letter word . . . But, then, so is play.
PAGAN KENNEDY, *Pagan Kennedy's Living*

My mother thinks I need a partner—a husband, to be more precise. She's enamored with her granddaughter, she thinks my career rocks, and she's certain that if I could just get that last element in place, my life would be perfect.

My mother thinks my sister needs a career—a fulfilling and lucrative career, to be more precise. My sister has a bright, energetic son, a boyfriend and a house in the country, and my mother is certain that if she could just get that last element in place . . .

I tell my mother not to worry, but she wants us to have It All.

Lately I've been thinking about It All. A journalist friend calls me periodically to ask if I think women can have It All. She's been asking various people this question for a long time. She's interested in the changing answer. What is It All?

My friend has never really broken it down for me, but I gather that It All consists of a solid relationship (preferably a marriage), tolerable children and a fulfilling career.

In the 1970s my friend decided, yes, women could have It All, but not all at once. In the 1980s she decided, yes, women could have It All, but perhaps only temporarily, sometime in our thirties.

When I was a kid we played a twisted little board game called "Life." You moved your little piece around the board on the path of life. You went to school, you got a job, you got married, you bought a house, you bought a few cars, you paid your taxes, you had children, and if you did all those things, in the right order, and if you avoided the pitfalls of getting laid off or going into debt or whatever, you won.

You won Life.

When my journalist friend calls, I usually tell her I don't know what women can or cannot have. Or I tell her about my mother and how she, too, wants me to have It All. Or I tell her which items on her list I think I have at that moment. But the truth is, her question bores me. I know plenty of miserable women who can lay claim to It All. And I know many others who are quite content without any of it.

We all know them. Still, we're quite fond of formulas for happiness: seven laws, six habits, four areas for improvement, five easy steps, three tests, 101 things to do, top ten reasons to do them, an eightfold path, cooks in three minutes, just add water.

I've tried to follow a fair number of these formulas. Their surface simplicity is compelling. I am intrigued, too, by ambiguity, by infinite possibilities, by the Cheshire Cat's grin.

But when it comes right down to it, I want a reliable recipe, a promise that everything will turn out just as it does at the end of the cooking show or the fairy tale. Perfect soufflé, happily ever after, simplicity. Never mind that a careful reading of any of the formulas always reveals more work than I bargained for (Step one: Make peace with the universe; add water, and chill for an eternity).

Once, while in the process of hiring a family law attorney, I noticed an *Alice's Adventures in Wonderland* poster on the lawyer's office wall. "Would you tell me, please, which way I ought to go from here?" Alice was asking.

"That depends a good deal on where you want to get to," said the Cat.

"I don't much care where—" said Alice.

"Then it doesn't matter which way you go," said the Cat.

"—so long as I get somewhere," Alice added as an explanation.

"Oh, you're sure to do that," said the Cat, "if you only walk long enough."

I smiled when I read this and thought it somewhat apropos. I didn't notice the poster again until I'd spent ten thousand dollars in legal fees and two and a half years in court following my smiling lawyer through a labyrinth of official incompetence. I had ignored her poster and imagined three simple tests, eight steps, a happy ending. But none of the tests were simple, none of the outcomes predictable. I got somewhere, all right. But nowhere near my intended destination.

❖

There have been years when I felt as if I had It All. A check in each of my journalist friend's three boxes. And there have been years when I could not lay claim to much of anything. But the funny thing is, when I focus on my most transcendent memories, those moments have very little to do with It All. And they have absolutely nothing to do with having It All at once.

You can have It All, yes. You can have a relationship, children and a career. And perhaps you will be content with It All. Lots of folks are. Following the formula certainly doesn't preclude happiness. Or maybe you will drive yourself crazy trying to keep It All together. It's hard to savor happily ever after when all the checked boxes need constant care, maintenance, rechecking. Or maybe you will long, in the middle of your busy day, for a fourth something that should have been on the list to begin with: December in Mexico, a rich inner life, dahlias in the kitchen sink.

Welfare Cinderella

They say money changes everything. It does and it doesn't. I spent seventy-five thousand dollars in twelve months, and all I have to show for it is a big purple couch and a little red car. Six years of accumulated single mom/college student debt didn't help. The student-loan sharks made off with a bunch of it. My landlord nabbed a few thousand in back rent. Still, you'd think I could tell you about at least one trip to Club Med . . . No, mine is a rags-to-riches-to-reality story in which the heroine and her daughter don't change their wardrobes a great deal.

I suppose the story begins in 1990 when, a week before my college freshman orientation, I walked into the welfare office and applied for a cash grant. At the time, applying for welfare seemed like an all-right thing to do; for the next six years, I got an AFDC check almost every month and promptly signed it over to my landlord. I learned, slowly, that there were a whole hell of a lot of Americans—from Newt Gingrich on down to my next-door neighbor who used to bang on my door screaming, "Whose responsibility is it to raise your damn kid, anyway?"—for whom my income source was not the least bit all right.

Maia and I never lived solely on that five-hundred dollar check from the state. When the government doesn't give a family enough to survive on at the beginning of the month and that family is still alive at the end of the month—well, obviously some fraud has taken place. My "fraud" was mostly legal; it consisted of a few thousand dollars a year in student loans, the odd work-study job, periodic checks begged from my grandmother and the Salvation Army, meals from various soup kitchens, Christmas presents from the local fire station giveaway, and about thirty dollars a week I made buying books and CDs at garage sales and pawning them off on resale shops at a minimal profit. My six years on welfare earned me a few prematurely gray hairs, but we got by.

Or maybe the story begins in late May of 1996. I'd just finished graduate school, hadn't landed a job, and my zine was still showing a loss. My cutoff notice from the welfare office was hanging on the wall next to my telephone when it rang at seven o'clock one morning. I was already up, on my way out the door to get to a local morning radio show to talk about being a welfare mama on the chopping block. Thinking it was my baby sitter calling, I answered the phone. A woman with a thick New York accent identified herself as my agent's partner and then told me matter-of-factly, "We just sold your book for one hundred thousand dollars."

Silence. I was trying to figure out who this crank caller was. "Hello?" the woman with the New York accent said after a minute. "You're kidding, right?" I said softly. Granted, I'd written the proposal and prayed for the money, but I don't like being teased. When I was about seven years old, my big sister and her friend told me that if I lay perfectly still on my stomach on top of the cab of the white pickup truck parked in our driveway, it would take off and fly me into outer space. I wasn't about to give this woman the same satisfaction my sister and her friend got when they came outside two hours later, laughing hysterically, as I lay perfectly still on top of that damn truck.

On the radio show later that morning, I announced I'd gotten the deal to write *The Hip Mama Survival Guide,* but I didn't mention the sum. Perhaps I'd heard it wrong. It was nearly noon by the time the reality of my new wealth had sunk in. Suddenly I felt like Cinderella. I called everyone I knew and a few people I didn't. I don't remember what I said to them. Probably something like, "And then this dude showed up with the glass slipper." After six years on welfare, one hundred thousand dollars minus the agent's cut and the illustrator's fee sounded like millions. I'd never be broke again. I could buy anything my heart desired. I could buy Maia anything her heart desired. I could pay back all my debts and live in the lap of luxury for eternity. The phrase "And they lived happily ever after . . ." might have crossed my mind.

I started writing down all the things I would buy when the check arrived. Shampoo and conditioner topped the list. I had never been a "responsible" poor person. I didn't clip coupons and, sometimes, we went out to dinner even as checks to the phone company bounced. When I was on welfare, I spent all the money in my pockets on whatever Maia or I wanted before I ever said "no." But I was an even less responsible rich person. When I had more money in my pockets, it simply took me longer to get to "no." For a year, I was a mama who only said "yes" ("One hundred dollars' worth of trinkets from the Statue of Liberty gift shop? Why not?"). For a year, I was a friend who wouldn't let anyone she knew get evicted ("Three-day notice? I'm on my way"). For a year, I was a writer-for-hire with a seriously snotty attitude ("Kiss my butt," I told an editor from a national magazine, who had always annoyed me, when he called with a dollar-a-word assignment).

The sobering bank statement didn't arrive until the following summer: I was on the verge of being totally broke again. The resale value of my couch and car were negligible. And, so, the "reality" part of my story begins. Even though the heroine is still sitting here in the same apartment in a nice part of town that the city planners nonetheless call an "area of persistent poverty," she's had a little bit of time to think about the real difference between rags and riches.

It's amazing to me how much kinder the world is to people with any disposable income to speak of. When my daughter had some cavities that needed to be filled this year, one phone call and one trip to the dentist did the trick— gone were the days of calling two dozen dentists and social service agencies in an attempt to get someone to take my Medi-Cal government insurance. When I bounced checks this year, my bank spoke of "oversights" and covered the difference—they used to speak of "irresponsibility" and charge me twenty-five bucks for the insult. When I was on deadline and my hard drive crashed, I drove over to Circuit City and bought a new computer. When Maia and I were driving to Los Angeles and we got tired of being in the car, we stopped in San Luis Obispo, booked a big pink room at the Madonna

Inn and took a horse and carriage ride around the lake. When a friend was crying and pleading with the driver as her car was being lifted onto a tow truck, I said "Shhh," handed the guy my secured credit card, and the ordeal was over.

It's true that you can't buy happiness, but you can buy an awful lot of peace and quiet. You can buy grace. Shit still happens when you have money; it's just a lot easier to deal with it.

Next to motherhood, being on welfare was the most radicalizing experience of my life. When you can't stop the cruelty of the world with a secured credit card, you can't avoid seeing the oppressive reality of it. And even if you know enough to appreciate the swiftness with which the cavities of people with bank accounts can be filled, it's easy to forget, while you're sitting in the waiting room reading *People*, the cluelessness that once denied you government insurance. My mother says that if I ever earn another big sum like that, I should put some money down on a house. But I probably won't. Houses are flammable, and, anyway, I bought the big purple couch on such a whim I forgot to measure my door. I ended up having to recruit two neighbor chicks to hoist it up over my second-floor balcony. I don't think we could get it out of here nearly as gracefully. But maybe we'll go to Club Med.

My Headache

Can someone please explain to me why it's more socially acceptable to be a twenty-something slacker with no kid than it is to be a stay-at-home mom? No, wait. I want that same person to explain to me why it is more socially acceptable to be the Air Force hack who drops cluster bombs on small countries than it is to be a mom who has a paying job. Honestly, every time I try to sit down to write about work and motherhood, I feel a headache coming on. It's a welfare-reform debate/"family values"/bring-home-the-bacon/you-only-get-to-be-a-dropout-till-you-get-knocked-up/fifties sitcom/Victorian/Puritan hangover kind of headache, if you know what I mean. It's a we-have-had-so-much-propaganda-rammed-down-our-throats-on-this-subject-that-I'm-not-sure-any-one-of-us-actually-knows-what-we-think kind of headache. It's a divide-and-conquer *how about let's not throw wads of guilt at each other* kind of headache. It's a bring-me-one-woman-who-actually-has-a-choice-in-the-matter-and-actually-wants-some-advice-on-what-to-do-with-her-free-time kind of headache. And Mamas, I have a limited amount of Advil at my disposal, so I'm only going to say this once: The kids are all right. Adaptable little creatures, they are.

The kids of women who work outside the home are all right. The kids of women who stay home to raise 'em up are all right. The kids of women like me who run businesses from their kitchen tables are all right. It would drive some of us into a mental institution if we home-schooled our kids and spent twenty-four/seven with them. It would drive some of us to Prozac if we had to work forty hours a week and have our kids in daycare.

As I write this, poor women are being pushed into the labor force on welfare-to-work programs while upper- and middle-class women are being cajoled out of it, ostensibly "for the sake of the children." Call me a commie, but I can only assume that, like everything else in America, all of this has more to do with "what's best for the stock market" than "what's best for the children."

Educated middle-class women are in a position to demand living wages and equal pay. Welfare-to-work "apprentices" often don't even get minimum wage. If you had your eye only on the bottom line, wouldn't *you* tell the equal-pay moms that they're neglecting their children and tell the cheap labor force to get some "personal responsibility"?

Did anyone else notice that the Dow Jones Industrial Average soared as soon as Bill Clinton signed the welfare-reform bill? And why wouldn't it have? Adding mothers to a slave labor force that already includes prisoners, immigrants and Third World women and children could only be good news for the economy.

Please don't believe the newspapers and the press secretaries when they try to tell us it is also good news for our families. It is vile, vile, vile news. What are we going to do about it?

Many feminist sisters throughout the history of the women's movement have fallen out over issues of home versus work, inner-life versus public life and so on. But let us not forget who defined these "separate spheres." Not us.

Plant Blue Roses

I just got an e-mail message from my friend Nanci. She's feeling "loserly" because she's more interested in her vegetable garden this morning than in "pursuing some aspect of her exciting career."

It's a common feeling, a part of the nasty little notion that persists in American culture—the notion that we are our jobs, that only those activities reflected in the GNP are worthwhile.

Of course, parenting is the ultimate nonmarket endeavor. Gardening usually is, too, like love and art.

In recent years, we've seen a proliferation of books and articles touting the idea that we should run every aspect of our lives, particularly our family lives, more like businesses. We read essays on lifestyle "downsizing," but the corporate metaphor doesn't quite fit. We can, and probably should, simplify our family lives, but we don't sit around charting the effect we're having on our children's productivity. We don't think to ourselves, "Well, this family would be a lot more profitable if we laid little Jimmy off and exported the job of being a preschooler to Mexico."

In *The Seven Habits of Highly Effective Families: Building a Beautiful Family Culture in a Turbulent World*, author Stephen R. Covey, who taught corporate America how to prosper with *The Seven Habits of Highly Effective People*, turns to parents, encouraging us to create a "family mission statement."

Others—*Mom, Inc.* and *Business Dad*—followed (just in case you needed an "org. chart" for your family). Can we all say fear of chaos? Or maybe it's just fear of life. Either way, it all makes me a little nauseated.

Our culture has managed to commodify everything from our sexuality to our souls. If I'm supposed to be the CEO of my family, where are my stockholders? Who is buying this crap?

"It's a measure of an insane age that we even need to point out that families are supposed to offer something besides effectiveness, that your mom or son doesn't actually have a mission," Tim Cavanaugh wrote in *Mother Jones*. "There's something creepy about a TV ad for minivans featuring a soccer mom shuttling the family around town while a voice-over describes her as the chief executive organizing her company."

Creepy indeed. (If it were up to me, CEOs would be more like moms, not the other way around.)

Most of us have jobs to make a living. When living itself belongs to the capitalist marketplace, we are all in deep trouble.

Nanci's e-mail message this morning is less creepy than pensive. She knows her vegetable garden belongs on the top of her list—with mothering her three kids and taking care of herself. But then there is that little pang of guilt, that little voice-over in her mind that says: *Nothing you are doing is*

advancing the GNP, nothing is affecting the Dow Jones Industrial
Average. In short: You're a loser! Get a mission, already.

When you hear that voice-over, recognize it for what it
is. And tend to your garden. Plant one, even if your only
space is like mine: an east-facing balcony with an overhang.

Aisha, a mom who contributes to hipmama.com, says:

> *For me, nurturing my flowers, herbs and other plants is*
> *like a link with the parts of me which need nurturing.*
> *It's also a wonderful, cyclical activity that inspires hope*
> *and dreams for the future. My eldest son loves to get*
> *out and dig in the dirt and has soaked up all kinds of*
> *gardening lore.*

Gardening can, of course, simply cause more guilt. Some
moms see it as just another item on their "to do" list. But if
like Aisha and Nanci, you find that the work of gardening
nurtures, make room for it in your nonmarket life.

If you're new to gardening and can't make heads or tails
of almanac instructions, have a talk with some wise and
friendly soul at your local nursery. Choose native plants that
will survive your space, climate and watering habits. These
will be your faithfuls. Then choose a few plants that seem
eccentric and hard to take care of.

Find a place for sage, lavender and rosemary. If you have
very small children playing in the garden, plant lamb's
ears—its woolly leaves are soft to the touch. Geraniums
never fail me. Plant a gardenia bush, and water it often. The

fragrant blooms will please you immeasurably. Find a place for basil; it will bring good luck. Tea roses are gorgeous. Put them in a big pot, and keep the soil damp. Plant sweet peas in the springtime, and save some pods for the following year. Learn to grow lettuce, carrots, leeks, corn, all kinds of squash and tomatoes. They will make you feel like you could survive an apocalypse.

And plant blue roses.

A garden reminds you that things are growing, even when you feel your life is at a standstill. And a garden reminds you that things take time, even when you feel your life is a nonstop catastrophe.

Morning Glory

Women are told not to be ambitious. Why not? Look at my morning glory in the back yard. When I put her in, the first thing she did was send out probes. The next year she took over the garden. I had to cut her back. I said, "Look, morning glory, do not kill my apple tree, my lemon tree, but you can have all this." Nature is very ambitious.

Z. BUDAPEST, *What is Enlightenment?*

Ambition is good. It's natural. When I talk about loafing, when I suggest taking a break from all those crazy market endeavors, I am not saying that it's time to go back to the ironing board. I'm saying you may find that it's time to go back to the drawing board. Our society channels our ambitions into "profitable" endeavors and ironing-board oppression. We need to explore our own ambitions, whatever they may be.

The modern Italian word *ozio* has been lost to English and most Latin-based languages. The best translation we have is leisure, or idleness. But *ozio* is not simple relaxation. It refers to the necessary meditative time that precedes a burst of creative energy. It allows time to jump off the "at-home" or career train and explore what else we might want. It is Gertrude Stein's loafing. It is the empty spaces necessary for reflection and refueling. *Ozio* does not go on indefinitely. Eventually our loafing leads to ideas. The creative energy kicks in, we send out probes, take over the garden.

When invited to name their dreams and ambitions, some of the mothers on hipmama.com shared these thoughts:

I want to go back to school and become either a marine biologist or wilderness guide.

I would like to run an inn with beautiful art and books everywhere.

I want to live the life I'm living now with a little more self-sufficiency each year. Maybe buy a milking goat. Buy this land, and convert our house to solar power.

Painting will always be my first love and personal outlet, but I'm tired of making a career out of art. I want to go back to school and study economics or become a stock analyst.

My dream is to be the information disseminator to the world. . . . I want to be a part of the Web revolution. The idea that everyone could find out about any subject they want, easy and quick, literally makes me giddy.

I want to be able to identify every plant and mushroom I see.

Name your dreams and ambitions, claim them as your own and build a family life that supports them.

Having children changes our lives dramatically. But children also come at times when we are looking for change. In her book *Summoning the Fates*, the spiritual leader Z. Budapest notes that women often get married and have children at auspicious "fate dates"—predestined developmental or astrological ages: nineteen, twenty-eight, thirty-three to thirty-four, and thirty-seven to thirty-eight.

If you have kids in your late twenties or early thirties, the change corresponds astrologically with the Saturn Return and with what Gail Sheehy calls "Catch-30" in her book *Passages*. It's the modern initiation into womanhood.

A book editor I know recently called to tell me she was leaving her job and moving to Virginia. "Why?" I wanted to know. At twenty-eight, she was a senior editor at a major publishing house in New York. Everyone I knew in publishing described her as "very ambitious." Perhaps she'd been offered an even better job?

"Well, no," she said cautiously. "I'm pregnant."

She had struggled with the decision to leave her job and lamented reactions from peers and from folks at her alma mater who made it clear she would no longer be considered the "model alum." But if she'd learned one thing in life, she told me, "it's that there is time to have more than one career and time to be a stay-at-home mom."

Another common experience is to be struck with our first strong ambitions after we have kids. I was a high school dropout and dedicated international bag lady when Maia was born. By the time she started first grade, I had an advanced degree and career plans that never crossed my mind pre-motherhood.

My ambition struck me almost immediately. For others, it builds slowly. "I got married very early, at nineteen, to a childhood sweetheart and quickly I started having babies, two sons, and my consciousness was just totally taken up with that," Z. Budapest told the magazine *What is Enlightenment?* "Things were just smooth and fine and clattered along until my Saturn cycle when I turned thirty, and then a big inner shift happened. This inner shift made me very restless and unhappy, and I started asking questions like, 'What is my role in life? What am I supposed to do?' I hadn't done anything yet. Even though I had two beautiful sons, I felt like I myself was not created."

One mother-friend made a similar remark a few years after her son was born and after she had endured a long and dangerous period of depression: "I no longer know why I am here on this earth."

This can be a frightening realization and admission, but it is also an acceptance of transformation. It's time to clear our lives of old ambitions and values that no longer seem to fit. It's time to make room for a new destiny.

Often we leave marriages or careers we no longer feel suited to. Often we become more focused on our chosen paths. Often, too, we set our sights on a new set of goals and ambitions. We get rid of the lives we've planned—or had planned for us—to make room for the new. We let go of negative perfectionism—the kind that focuses on inadequacy.

And we get into positive perfectionism—the kind that recognizes and affirms our talents. (Sounds a lot like good parenting, huh? But here we are focusing on ourselves as well as our kids.) The point is not change for the sake of change. We needn't throw away the decent and supportive people and things in our lives in some whacked housecleaning frenzy. The point instead is to accept the time of transformation and become more ourselves.

Here are some questions we can ask ourselves during times of transition in our lives:

- Where am I feeling burdened, restricted and limited in my life?
- What in my life makes me feel competent?
- Where am I wasting time, energy, money?
- What do I enjoy?
- What is my favorite time of day? Why?
- Where is my passion?
- In what areas of my life am I still living out someone else's "shoulds"?
- Do I see motherhood as all-giving, or can I make room for learning to mother myself as well as others?
- In what ways do I feel like a kid bull-shitting in a grown-up world?
- In what ways do I feel as if I am juggling dissonant parts of my life?
- Which of these balls can I set down? What am I afraid of in doing so?
- What do I feel I have "sacrificed" for my current work/family/lifestyle?

Still More Questions Than Answers

"When do you find time to write, paint, express your creative self?" I get asked this question constantly.

Finding time for oneself isn't a new dilemma. In 1838 Harriet Beecher Stowe tried to make light of our predicament, writing out a little conversation with herself:

"Come Harriet," said I, as I found her tending one baby and watching two others just able to walk, "where is that piece for the Souvenir which I promised the editor I would get from you? You have only this one day left to finish it, and have it I must."

"And how will you get it, friend of mine? . . . You will at least have to wait till I get housecleaning over and baby's teeth through."

"As to housecleaning, you can defer it one day longer; and as to baby's teeth, there is to be no end to them, as I can see . . . "

By 1841, she knew it was getting more serious:

Our children are just coming to the age when everything

depends on my efforts. They are delicate in health, and nervous and excitable and need a mother's whole attention. Can I lawfully divide my attention by literary efforts? . . . If I am to write, I must have a room to myself, which shall be my room.

When Virginia Woolf wrote *A Room of One's Own* in 1928, most of the prominent women writers and artists of the century before had had a measure of economic independence and privacy and, like Woolf, were childless (Jane Austen, Emily Brontë, Charlotte Brontë, George Eliot . . .).

When Tillie Olsen wrote *Silences* in 1963, the situation was changing, but childless women still dominated the list of well-known women artists (Willa Cather, Isak Dinesen, Eudora Welty, Zora Neale Hurston, Anaïs Nin, Flannery O'Connor, Georgia O'Keefe, Billie Holiday, Frida Kahlo and Woolf, to name a few).

By the time Alice Walker wrote her 1976 essay "One Child of One's Own: A Meaningful Digression Within the Work(s)," feminism, washing machines and birth control had changed everything. Or had it? Now our lists of women artists and writers included heartening numbers of mothers— Walker, of course, and Olsen; Toni Morrison, Maya Angelou, Adrienne Rich, Alta, Paula Gunn Allen . . .

But our struggles had not changed drastically enough. In 1976, Jane Lazarre noted:

The meaning of work and the need to learn to insistently be an artist in the midst of family is what I am now and always trying to understand, and after each understanding

to painstakingly, always with great attention to detail,
structure my time . . . I feel still caught in the middle,
between that time when women will be able to work and
have children and love . . . and the past, the physical and
emotional crampedness. I have my desk in the middle of
the living room and the apartment is mine at least four
hours each day (not enough) but emotionally, I sneak off
into a corner to grab an idea and promise to transform it
into something whole.

And this is where we remain—caught between the tides, between that time when women will be able to work and have children and love . . . and the past.

In the middle of this incomplete revolution, we see mothers redesigning life in every imaginable way—some of us work and express our creative selves in school-day-length spurts; some have found a working rhythm that thrives amid children's shrieks and giggles; some of us take a year, or five or ten years "off," surrendering completely to motherhood and planning, in time, to return to our other work(s); some of us accept that our projects will each take four times as long as they might have when we were childless; some of us use daycare and baby sitters more than others; some rise before the sun; some do not rest until long after midnight.

When do I find time to write, paint, express my creative self? Often I do not. I have lost more stories than I would like to admit. Some mornings I wake up with a notebook next to my pillow. There are just a few words at the top of the page and the squiggle mark from the pen I dropped when I fell asleep. But other times I do find the time. And, truth be told, it was as a mother that I found my way into writing at all. I neglect housework. I trade overnight baby-sitting duties with mother-friends. And I envision a new aesthetic in books and art, one in which you can hear the children screaming right through the middle.

Room in the Dark, Part One
(Notes from Cyberspace)

DANIELLE

I was just wondering if there were any other creative mamas out there with non-sleeping, high-need little folk in the house. I'm feeling really incomplete—haven't been able to write for a solid year, and even let my journaling slip, BAD idea! I am also missing the kind of uninterrupted laziness it takes to get a really good idea going. Any suggestions? Hallie will only sleep for a half-hour or so without me at night, so working really late isn't much of an option. I am starting to get deeply depressed. Help!

KIM

I have done some work since my kids were born (three years and seven months) but definitely not as much as I did before I was a mom. I actually asked poet Anne Waldman about how she handled working after her son was born, and she suggested keeping a journal, notebook, or whatever nearby all the time and jotting short things down, especially about the kids, little haikus, descriptions, etc. so that I could go back and fill in more later. This helped some, although sometimes I ended up balancing a journal on the back of a sleeping baby in my lap. I do stay up to work late sometimes when my hubby works second shift and the kids are in bed, but I figure I can always get the heavy duty novel writing done in a couple of years when the kids are in school.

SARAH

I have struggled with this for eight years now. I have no real answer, but two observations: Guilt will kill any creativity you have left after creating and nurturing a human life. Writing for five minutes or ten minutes really often can become meditative—I have learned to get into my writing head really, really fast. And isn't this journaling? Don't be too strict about your definitions—what's REAL writing and what's not good enough. One book I love suggests writing poems and giving them away immediately so that you never see them again. What a freeing experience.

BETH

I find that with my time so interrupted I just can't clear my head and get into a state of mind that is conducive to being creative. I've taken to loading the car with books, magazines, paper, pen and music. When my son falls asleep in the car I find a nice place to chill and relax. It's just nice to be in the car basically alone while he sleeps. No chores staring me in the face, no distractions. I'm just starting to push out a few (and I mean a few) creative things. It's a slow process for me, but I feel my mind is closer to being able to do something more creative now than when my son was younger.

LILA

As a writer and painter, I've always had trouble transitioning in and out of creative periods—most of my best work has been done when I had loads of uninterrupted time to work. I used to be notorious among my friends for canceling plans or not showing up at parties if I was in the middle of working on a painting or a piece of writing. I could sleep and eat when I wanted to and work the rest of the time. I've been thinking about how Ernest Hemingway (I know, hardly a hip mama!) wrote five pages a day, no matter what. Sometimes they took an hour, sometimes all day. Sometimes they sucked and had to be pitched later. But at least they were written. Don't know if something like that would work for me.

SIERRA

My son is three months old and already I think about the designs in clay I'm not making. Just this week I allowed myself to let housey stuff be left undone and dipped into short sessions. I noticed that even though I wasn't making much, the gaps between hands-on time allowed me to think more about what I was doing. I'd do a little and then muse over the designs as I breast-fed, folded laundry, whatever. It felt important just to make token attempts at keeping the creative side alive.

JULIE

NEVER, NEVER, NEVER give up your art in order to dedicate your time to taking care of the babes or the house or work! I mean it! You still need that for YOU! I got some crazy notion in my head that I had to give it up, and I was WRONG. I miss it terribly, and am trying to bring it back into my life. It's so hard to do when you quit cold turkey. But, I will and I am worth it. So are you! Take care of yourselves . . .

Small Stones

Whether I'm out on tour giving talks or at home reading my e-mail, I hear from dozens of mothers every day. They are mothers from all over the world with different lifestyles and different family structures, but they tell an all-too-similar story. They are mothers who are, by all accounts, working their asses off—all accounts, that is, but their own.

One mother who writes an important column on women's issues recently confessed to me that she knew she "ought to be doing more." She wrote about the effects of welfare reform but took part in no political actions to reverse it. She reported on the lack of affordable child care in her state, but couldn't offer to care for her neighbor's children. She wrote about domestic violence, and had once harbored an acquaintance who was hiding from an abusive partner, but she was afraid to open her home to strangers. "If I'm not a part of the solution . . . " she started to tell me. But, of course, she is a part of the solution. Her column informs. It inspires others who can be part of the solution in their own small or grand ways.

Another friend e-mailed recently expressing some embarrassment about having her local radio show broadcast internationally from hipmama.com. To her the show did not quite measure up to the other material on the site. I e-mailed back a paragraph from Alice Walker's *Anything We Love Can Be Saved*.

> *It has become a common feeling, I believe, as we have watched our heroes falling over the years, that our own small stone of activism, which might not seem to measure up to the rugged boulders of heroism we have so admired, is a paltry offering toward the building of an edifice of hope. Many who believe this choose to withhold their offerings out of shame.*
>
> *This is the tragedy of our world.*

Remember: As women, as mothers, we cannot *not* work. Put aside your ideas that your work should be something different or grander than it is. In each area of your life—in work, art, child-rearing, gardening, friendships, politics, love and spirituality—do what you can do. That's enough. Your small stone is enough.

Throw Away the Iron

You can live with nomads or hunter-gatherers, maybe, or become a nun with nothing but a cell to distract you from the day-long excitement of prayer. Or maybe you can make a vow that no more than an hour in any day may be spent on housework—and keep it. This really would be the end of civilization as we know it.

GERMAINE GREER, *The Whole Woman*

Raid kills on contact, kills with residual action. Shout quickly penetrates stains. Clorox Clean-Up kills 99 percent of household germs in thirty seconds. Ultra Sunlight dish detergent fights bacteria. O-Cel-O anti-bacterial sponges resist odors and kill germs. Playtex latex gloves promise the wearer total "control and security." All are hazardous to humans and domestic animals and should be kept out of the reach of children.

For just $29.94, you too can arm yourself to do mythic battle of a vaguely sexual nature with the devious forces that threaten your home.

But you'll have to be willing to invest a little more than

thirty seconds into the war effort. Everything here may be concentrated, fast-acting, powerful, long-lasting, cutting, penetrating and generally deadly, but there is literally no end to the amount of it you can scrub into your floors, basin, tub, tiles, clothes, dishes, windows and walls.

And not all the cleaning agents are so sexy. One glass cleaner advertises having "all the power of vinegar." The person who can tell me why I shouldn't just buy vinegar at a quarter of the price can also probably explain the concept behind white carpets. Are we in heaven yet?

Housework, done properly, can kill you.

It can also cause depression, inertia and the dreaded dish-pan hands.

If you're as tired of housework as I am, repeat with me after Germaine: *No more than an hour in any day may be spent on housework.*

What? You can't do all your housework in an hour? Of course you can't! Housework is designed to absorb every waking moment you spend in your home. But laundry can cushion feet as well as wall-to-wall carpeting can. When you run out of clean dishes, you can always order pizza. And who says you and your kids can't wear the same pair of jeans every day? Do take out the garbage, but beyond the basics—screw it. As comedian Phyllis Diller says, "Cleaning the house while the kids are still growing is like shoveling the sidewalk before it stops snowing." If your other family members don't like it, they'll learn to pick up your slack. Goddess knows you've picked up their slack from time to time.

❖

When a friend's kids were two and four, an aunt bought them a plastic iron and ironing board for Christmas so that they could play housewives. The kids set up the board, got a couple of cups from the kitchen, pulled up two chairs and had a tea party. They were delighted with the gift, but they wondered why the table was so high and the kettle so oddly shaped. Having never laid eyes on a real iron and board, they didn't quite get it.

This is as it should be.

"Have you thrown away your iron yet?" someone asked me when I was a new mother, as if it were a veritable rite of passage.

Little kids are messy creatures. They don't need to be filthy, but they're disheveled. An iron is no match for the chaos that is life with young children; it's just a household hazard.

Next time you pick your kid up from school or daycare, take a good look around. All the kids are a mess. The only difference between the kids whose parents iron and those who do not is that the ironers' kids have nasty little burns on their arms or foreheads. They're really no better pressed.

My Cleaning Goddess

A few years ago, finally having an income over the poverty level, I decided it was time to get some therapy. I was twenty-six years old, I'd lived in California most of my life and I'd never sat on a therapist's couch. It seemed obvious to me and to most people I knew that this lack of therapy was the root of all my problems.

Proud that I was finally on the road to "recovery," I paid sixty dollars a week to go and talk to a nice lady who let me whine and project and vent and do headstands whenever I wanted. She offered me her wisdom, and it made the world seem a bit more tolerable. But every night, I still had to do the dishes. And every morning, I woke up thinking, "Man, I have to buy a vacuum cleaner one of these days." When I got home after therapy, there was always a load of laundry waiting for me.

And then one day, I had a dream.

I had heard about these dreams from therapized friends all my life—those rare moments when, after spending a certain number of hours sorting through old issues, we catch a clear glimpse into our psyches and emerge with a revelation. This was my dream: *maid service*. And my revelation: *Sixty dollars a week could buy me a clean house, and then I wouldn't need the therapy.* I had caught a clear glimpse into my own psyche and had seen myself for who I really was: a slob who couldn't stand a mess.

I picked up the local weekly newspaper, scanned the "home services" section of the classifieds and answered an ad for "Simply Clean."

I canceled my therapy session scheduled for the following Wednesday, and instead Anne came over, two-year-old daughter in tow.

She did my dishes. She scrubbed my kitchen floor. She vacuumed. She put away the videos scattered around the television. She cleaned the bathtub. She atomized the Kool-Aid stain on the ceiling I'd been meaning to deal with since Maia was four. She dusted.

We listened to music, our kids played and I did the laundry.

Within three hours, my house was spotless. I wrote her a check for fifty dollars and felt saner than I had all year.

My therapized friends think it's terribly bourgeois of me to have a cleaning lady, and at first I blushed when they stopped by while Anne was scrubbing my bathtub, but I am learning to live with my shame.

Perhaps I could still use the therapy to explore how I became such a disorganized person, but for now I am content with the peace an empty kitchen sink inspires in me. For now, my inner child squeals with joy as I walk barefoot across a newly vacuumed floor.

I was pretty sure Anne would laugh at me when, after she'd been coming for a few months, I confided my housecleaner-as-therapist theory.

"Oh yeah," she said matter-of-factly. "I'm actually in training to be a healer. And this is a part of it. I'm helping you clear away your old stuff. That's what healing is about."

Far out, I thought. *The things they don't teach you in twenty-six years in California.*

Housework Versus Homecare

When I was growing up in the 1970s, *housewife* was a dirty word. Listening to the record *Free to Be You and Me,* my sister and I learned that mommies hated housework, that daddies hated housework and that Carol Channing hated housework, too. With good reason. Historically speaking, housework has been indentured servitude for women. Okay. I guess you could say I have a thing about housework.

But there's a difference between housework, which is thankless, and homecare. When we do homecare, it's because we want to, not because we have to. We take care of our living spaces so that they'll look wicked and feel like home.

Sometimes the idea of home as the place where we are safe and cared for seems nostalgic or one-sided. It describes the husband's experience of being cared for by his housewife. But we can also create our own living spaces where we feel safe as women.

In the age of the telephone, the television and the Internet, the walls between our homes and the outside world are weakened. Distant wars take place in our living rooms. Stalkers need only know our log-in names to harass us. And because domestic violence is still so prevalent, statistically speaking, we are safer in dark alleys than we are in our own homes.

If you've ever been in an abusive relationship, then you know that housework is what you do to keep your partner happy and avoid an attack. Homecare is what you do when you sweep him out the door.

Housework is what you do when you wash the television screen with Windex even though you don't watch the thing yourself. Homecare is what you do when you designate a certain time of day when the TV is always off—or better yet, throw it out into the middle of the street.

We care for our homes by making them places where we can be ourselves. If this means we keep them in varying states of chaos, that is what we need. If this means our homes are tidy, but we can write our dreams on the walls, that is what we need. If we can only be ourselves in homes that are spotless all of the time, then that is what we need. Caring for our spaces doesn't have to be drudgery. If there is something you need done in your house that you can't stand to do yourself, please hire a neighborhood kid to come do it. A couple of hours a week isn't likely to break you.

When we stop doing drudgery housework and start doing homecare, our homes become nurturing places where we and our family-folk can build strong selves capable of walk-ing tall in the outside world.

Notes from the Couch

I drive a reliable, geeky car. I live in the "parent 'hood." I drink cheap beer. But I have my priorities: I have grand, silly, expensive, luxuriantly comfortable couches. I am writing from one right now. If there were another seven feet in my apartment I would buy another one. My first giant purple velvet couch wouldn't fit through the front door when I bought it. I wasn't discouraged. I tied a rope around it and hauled it up over the second-floor balcony.

Couches can be pricey pieces, but only beds rival couches in their utility. In the living room, they introduce guests to who we are. In the family room, we nurse new babies on them and talk to our children as well as our friends and lovers on them. We sneak naps on them. We watch the latest government scandal on TV from them, and they give us comfort from this deranged world. A good couch will be formal on some days, a place where we can sit and entertain new in-laws, and so comfortable on other days we can't imagine ever getting out of our pajamas.

My friend Mary, a pregnant mother of a toddler, on the couch:

Relaxing has become a very bizarre event in my life these

days with being the mom of a sixteen-month-old and six months pregnant with the next. At seven in the evening, just after I put Jake to bed, I collapse on the couch and stare at Unsolved Mysteries *until I recover from the afternoon, which can take up to an hour. This feels incredibly mindless—I relax, I even cry sometimes (when people on the show are reunited after thirty years of being torn apart by family break-ups and the like). It's a nice release. I also find that wandering alone, taking the dog for a walk after dark, spending an hour in the bookstore are good ways of relaxing, but the best is lying on the couch. Before my first pregnancy, I don't think I ever found lying on the couch interesting. Though I am a cartoonist, my mind just isn't there to come up with the jokes right now, so I oil paint instead, which is invigorating and relaxing at the same time. Also, I will occasionally have a pedicure at one of those nail salons as it helps me feel somewhat beautiful at a time when my body image is suffering. Then I come home and lay on the couch.*

Get in touch with your couch. If yours is lumpy, short, propped up with a board or covered in a hideous puke-green fabric, take a good look at your priorities. And next windfall, get yourself a grand, silly, luxuriant, comfortable couch.

The Sticker Lady

One winter when Maia was having a particularly hard time getting herself out of bed and ready for school on time, I decided to implement a little sticker-and-prize system ("positive reinforcement" as it is euphemistically called). I usually try to avoid this kind of thing. To me, positive reinforcement is "You go, girl." Once stickers and prizes are involved, it's bribery. But I was desperate, and in this case I figured the end would justify the means. When Maia and I talked about it, she agreed that the incentive program would help her remember to get up when I woke her up, not to play with her hamsters until after she'd gotten dressed, not to stare blankly into the mirror while she was supposed to be brushing her teeth and so forth. The plan was that she would earn a sticker every day she was on time to school, and once she had amassed thirty stickers, she would get the skates I had been planning to buy her anyway. It seemed simple. All I had to do was buy the supplies, and we'd be on our way toward a springtime of graceful mornings.

I marched into the little school supply store in our neighborhood feeling very organized and picked out some sparkly bug stickers and a cute calendar that featured colorful pictures of New York City.

"What are you doing?" the woman behind the counter wanted to know as I set the stickers and calendar down in front of her. I casually explained my plan to her.

"So she gets one sticker for each day?" the woman asked.

"Yes," I said. "Every day she's on time."

"What does she have to do in the morning in order to be on time?"

"Well," I said. "I guess she has to get out of bed, get dressed, brush her teeth and hair, wash up, eat breakfast . . . you know, the standard . . . "

"And she only gets one sticker for all that?"

At this point I was starting to get just a wee bit nervous. "Yeah," I said.

"So she gets penalized for the whole morning if she forgets to do one thing?"

"I guess. The point is she's supposed to get to school on time."

The woman shook her head. I could tell she had no intention of ringing up my purchases, but being new to the whole sticker-and-prize system, I thought I should hear her out.

"What you have to do," the woman explained very seriously, "is you have to give her a sticker for each part of the morning. Let's say she gets up on time. Sticker. Let's say she brushes her teeth, washes her face and brushes her hair in a timely fashion. Sticker. Let's say she eats her breakfast and gets her backpack on. Sticker. You can get smaller stickers if money is the issue."

"All right," I said. It all seemed a little more complex than what I'd originally had in mind, but this woman seemed to know what she was talking about. I thanked her for the tips and pushed my stickers and calendar a little closer to her.

"Now," she said, sitting down on the stool behind the counter. "What are the stickers worth?"

"Worth?"

"Yes, yes," she said. "The stickers have to have a monetary value."

"Well, she gets the skates after thirty on-times, like I said."

"All right. Then let's say the skates cost twenty dollars, she needs ninety stickers for a pair of skates," the woman quickly punched some buttons on her calculator. "Round up. We're looking at twenty-five cents per sticker."

Perhaps she didn't notice that I was holding my head in my hands at this point, because she went on. And on.

"Lady," she was saying. "This calendar is *way* too small for what you need. Three stickers for the morning routine. Three stickers for the afternoon routine. Three stickers for the nighttime routine. And, of course, with my children I have their teachers give them okays for every day they get through the school routine. Every sticker is worth twenty-five cents, five okays are worth a half-hour of TV time, they can buy extra TV time at four stickers or one dollar per hour. If they want time on the Internet that's one dollar or four stickers for every hour if it's for fun, two stickers or fifty cents for every hour if it's educational . . . "

I nodded, pushed the calendar and stickers right up to the back edge of the counter, and asked if I could please just buy these things. "I was just trying to make our lives," I managed, "a little bit simpler."

She shook her head. "You'll regret this," she said gravely as she rang up my stickers and calendar.

I took my little plastic bag of supplies and slouched away.

Maia managed to get up and off to school most mornings after that, with the help of a single sticker. And our mornings became, if not graceful, at least a bit easier.

But every once in a while, as I am affixing one of the sparkly bug stickers to Maia's colorful New York City calendar, I think of the sticker lady and her children, and I wonder if anything was ever meant to be that complicated.

Uninterruptible

*Where are we going to learn to use these spiritual
weapons? The only answer that we can see is in retreat
houses, where we can spend eight days every year and
monthly days besides. . . . It is certainly a dream for the
future—a retreat house by the sea. . . . A retreat house
with a farming community attached where food can be
raised and for all the retreatants, who will be workers
and poor people from our bread lines, mothers. . . . There
would almost have to be a nursery attached where these
mothers could leave their children for a week . . .*

DOROTHY DAY, *Meditations*

It breaks my heart when mothers tell me they do not have
the time to take care of themselves, do not have the energy
to find support, or do not have the freedom to drop everything once in a while and do something for themselves. We
still do not have the retreat houses Dorothy Day imagined in
1943. But I watch these mothers. I know them. They are the
same women who always have time to help a first grader
with her homework, who always conjure up the energy to
feed a hungry infant in the middle of the night, and who are

always available to drop everything on a moment's notice and rush to a schoolyard where their toddler has fallen off a play structure or skinned his knee. We don't have a lot of time or energy to spare, but we are masters of making time, of conjuring energy, of demanding accommodation when our children need us. We have to be. But what about when *we* need us? Ah, then it's a different story. Suddenly phrases like "of course" and "I'll be right there" turn into phrases like "I wish I could" and "maybe next week."

In her book *Silences*, Tillie Olsen wrote: "More than in any other human relationship, overwhelmingly more, motherhood means being instantly interruptible, responsive, responsible." But with time, we become accustomed to this state of perpetual responsiveness. Many of us even begin to find comfort in the interruptions, knowing we will not be allowed to follow a train of thought or flow of events too far, that a sudden wail from the nursery or paper airplane whizzing past will soon bring us back to the here and now. We adjust our schedules to accommodate the inevitable interruptions. We learn to rinse the conditioner out of our hair in five seconds and jump out of the shower to resolve a conflict that has erupted over a Pokémon card. We choose books with three-page chapters so that we can read in short intervals. We conform our whole lives to the mold of responsible motherhood. We get used to it, but it is no way to live all of the time.

"I recommend that every woman get a divorce," radio commentator Andrea Pearson joked when she got her first taste of joint custody after her separation. "Because even though you're on your own for two weeks at a stretch, you get every other weekend all to yourself, in sweet solitude. I never got that kind of quality alone time when I was married." There is some truth in every joke. But we don't have to go through a divorce to demand that alone time. Maybe you cannot take every other weekend off in sweet solitude. One full day each month and several long weekends a year may be enough. However long you can afford to take, the important thing is that you take it, and take it without guilt.

My friend Susan gives her husband a taste of single parenthood one day a week and a full week once a year during her convent retreats. To nourish her creative life, she has found that she does need a room of her own. At the convent, she gets a tiny room with a view of the courtyard, a small bed, a desk, a closet, a sink and a window.

It's cheaper than staying at a hotel. It's also more peaceful. I go and lock myself in, and I write and take naps and in general get blissed out. I love having my own bed, just my own plate and cup to wash. Everything is very simple. The place is loaded with contemplative spots: a seating place that is made of packed earth and shaped like a womb that you can sit inside, a gorgeous small straw-bale house called "The Hermitage," where you can go to be really alone; plus little logs and benches and gardens and paths and a courtyard with a little fountain and trees; meditation rocks and pebbles and bells and incense and candles everywhere. Deer roam the place freely. There's an absolutely gorgeous chapel with this tree hung with gold origami cranes. The sisters who run it are cooler than cool; one of them gives a monthly workshop on the spiritual art of paper making where she makes paper out of leaves and flowers. It's amazing.

"[W]omen who are tired, temporarily sick of the world, who are afraid to take time off, afraid to stop, wake up already!" Clarissa Pinkola Estés writes in *Women Who Run with the Wolves.* "Lay a blanket over the banging gong that cries for you to infinitely help this, help that, help this other thing. It will be there to uncover again, if you wish it so, when you come back."

What you do with your time away is up to you. You do not have to plan anything at all. You may want to go to the mountains or to a strange city. Or you may want to stay close to home. Do not force yourself into a strict agenda beyond being good to yourself, responsive to yourself.

Perhaps you will spend your time sleeping—for twelve hours at a stretch. Perhaps you will spend the afternoon riding your bicycle around town without any particular destination. Perhaps you will spend a whole weekend lying in the sun, knitting, going to the movies, having coffee with an old friend, wandering around in the rain without an umbrella, picking wildflowers, reading, sitting at a bar, or going shopping and trying on clothes you know you will never buy.

Allow yourself to follow the day wherever it takes you. Allow yourself to become mesmerized by the flow of events, by the uninterruptedness of it all. Perhaps one thing will lead to another and another and another, and by day's end you will feel as if you have lived a whole life. More likely you will notice, as the sun is setting, that you have not accomplished a single tangible thing.

Whatever you end up doing with your time, know that it is exactly what you need to be doing. This day, or weekend, or week away is not a one-shot deal. It must become a regular part of your life. So if you meant to spend your day climbing a mountain and instead found yourself reading a thick novel at the funky cafe with the elk head mounted on the wall, do not decide, on your way home, that you have been lazy. It doesn't matter. You can climb the mountain next time. Or not.

Escape to New York

As soon as I step out of the JFK airport terminal into the muggy dawn, I feel disoriented. It's not that the air is thick with the smells of mildew and rats, although it is.

It's not that I'm immediately accosted by half a dozen cab drivers, though I am. It's not even that I'm tired and nauseated after a cheap red-eye flight across the country. No, my confusion this morning has more to do with the new identity zone I am stepping into than with my particular geographical location. I'm on a week-long furlough—I left Maia back in California—and with only my own feelings to consider, I can't even remember how to make a decision as simple as this: subway or car service?

In Oakland, Maia and I live a mostly quiet life. My hot-pink hair and the fact that, at twenty-seven, I am at least a decade younger than most of the other moms at Maia's school hint at a more exciting life than we actually lead. We hang out at Safeway. We feed the cat. I write while she's at school. I help her with her homework. So, what happens after we have grown accustomed to our mama-ness? Even comfortable with it? What happens after years of always being interruptible? After we've designed our lives and trained our senses to be always responsive and responsible, what happens when we suddenly land, alone, at JFK and realize that no one really cares how we get to Manhattan?

I end up in a taxi, and I am still a little queasy when I finally get to my friend's apartment on the Lower East Side. I ring his doorbell once and then curl up in his doorway, using the Hello Kitty duffel bag I borrowed from my daughter as a pillow. I probably should have tried harder to wake him, but it's been ages since I rested like this in a doorway, and for the first time in seven years, I can.

It is still early morning, and few people are out on the street. A woman approaches me cautiously and leans down to ask if I need a fix. "You okay?" she wants to know. "'Cause we can go see my man Raul." When I wake up I feel youth-sick and oddly exhilarated. I ring my friend's doorbell, and when he hears I've been outside since sunrise he looks at me with a mixture of pity and concern. "Have you lost your mind?" I just laugh. I can't say I haven't.

On this first day, I am cautious. My first book is being published in the spring and I have several business meetings and expense-account lunches to focus on. And although (according to my friend, Dave) I look like a cross between a rock star and a housewife, by my standards I am dressed up. I amuse myself, uttering simple sentences: "Sure, I'll have another beer"; "If I don't come back tonight, I'll just see you tomorrow"; and, my favorite, "No, I have no interest in going to see the Statue of Liberty." (When I was here with Maia last year, we were poster children for New York tourism—twenty-dollar T-shirts and all.)

By the second day, I am giddy. I stop by an old boyfriend's

apartment at random hours—mostly for the thrill of not having to listen for the pitter-patter of little footsteps coming down the hall. He's a guy I lived with in wilder days—when he was in high school and I was the mod party-girl dropout. Now when I scream in his bed, I all but forget he's a Narcotics Anonymous convert and I'm in the PTA.

I call Maia to check in, half-hoping she will offer me something to feel guilty about, or at least some grounding thoughts. But she doesn't. She hates the city. She is glad she didn't have to come. "It's dark in New York," she says. "And stinky." She is having a blast; the tooth fairy brought her five bucks, and she doesn't need a thing from me. This isn't the first time we've been apart, but I've always stayed in Oakland when Maia went off for the weekend. And when I'm on home turf, the circle I travel in is, admittedly, a maternal ghetto. Most of my friends in Oakland have children, so even when I do not have my own baby sitter to relieve, I find myself rushing home from concerts as if my Honda were on the verge of turning into a pumpkin. I spend the days when she is gone catching up on work, and even when I go out to Club Red, I leave before last call. I only stop for one drink after a Lauryn Hill show. At home I remain in mama-mode: always prepared to respond to an urgent telephone call, checking my messages at least twice a day and rarely allowing my blood alcohol level to creep above the legal limit.

By Thursday, I begin to lose track of days and nights altogether. I'm sometimes tipsy, but mostly I'm high on the uninterruptedness of it all. I am mesmerized by the flow of time and events—one thing leads to another and another and another—and even when I stop long enough to eat a piece of pizza, no paper airplane noses onto my plate to bring me back to reality.

Skidding into adolescent oblivion, I get a CD-sized tattoo on my shoulder at a shop where they blare Violent Femmes like it's 1985. I fall head-over-heels in love with a woman I barely know. A woman with stripes in her hair. At a dinner party, someone asks if my daughter knows I will be coming home with the tattoo, and I remember that when I got my first one at sixteen, someone asked if my mother knew.

At one in the morning in New Jersey, after an Ani DiFranco show, I hear that the trains have stopped running, and it doesn't even occur to me to worry about how I'm going to get back to Manhattan. Without a little kid whining about our predicament, without any baby sitter to relieve, I have time to wait for luck to kick in. I get back. Of course I get back. I hitch a ride with a busload of wasted Brits who came to see Bob Dylan scratch out a few tunes after Ani left the stage. I stay up all night blaring music and smoking with a friend in her elegant apartment on the Upper West Side. At six in the morning I crash and sleep until noon. I forget to eat.

One morning—I don't know which one—as I'm parting from a new friend after spending all night in her tiny East Village apartment talking about hair dye, Beth Lisick prose poems and bisexuality, I am filled with a strange feeling of deceitfulness when I realize this new friend knows that I was born under the sign of Cancer, knows that the subway signs in this town make me think of Lawrence Ferlinghetti books, knows that I prefer black licorice to red, but knows nothing of my daughter and the left front tooth she lost last week.

That afternoon, I confide my identity crisis to a woman at a bar on the Lower East Side who bears an uncanny resemblance to Nina Hagen. "You're not regressing," the woman assures me. "This is just life without kids."

"You mean, when people don't have kids, they act like this all the time?" I ask, incredulous. "And you don't get tired?"

She smiles. "Well," she begins slowly as she orders another drink, "you do get tired, but then you just sleep. And, of course, at some point there are health concerns. And if you've got a job or a career or something—" I just stare at her, trying to imagine what my life would be like without anyone to interrupt me, without having to be responsive, responsible. When I was eighteen and pregnant, I used to joke that I was having a baby to keep myself out of trouble. And now I realize it was true. Here I thought I'd grown up in seven years, and all I'd done was find another use for my ability to function without sleep.

I wonder what my life would be like without my daughter's all-encompassing presence, and I am somewhat comforted to realize that without the grounding effect she has on me, I'd probably just go get myself knocked up.

PART III

The Mama Blues

Only to the extent that we expose ourselves over and over to annihilation can that which is indestructible be found in us.

PEMA CHÖDRÖN, *When Things Fall Apart*

If It's All You Can Do to Get Out of Bed in the Morning, Just Get Out of Bed

The most desolate season of my motherhood began the day I came home from a long weekend conference in Montana to news that I was on my way to family court for the thirteenth time. After twelve trips to family court, you might think I'd have been used to it, used to the stark language of legal papers that negotiated my daughter's fate with all the passion of a used car deal, and reduced her parents to "petitioner" and "respondent." But I don't know if you ever get used to those things.

It had been over a year since my daughter's father and I had finally settled some of our differences and embarked on a hard-won truce that I honestly believed would be lasting. So the news of a thirteenth lawsuit hit me hard. I got out the old combat boots I used to wear to family court, but my feet had grown a half-size and they no longer fit. For the first time in my life, when attacked, I didn't feel like fighting back. Instead I read Joan Didion: "The heroine is not as optimistic as she once was."

I tried to immerse myself in work and in the mundane daily tasks of motherhood: mac and cheese, shuttling the kid back and forth to school and martial arts, running baths with the water temperature just so, not too hot, not too cold, but even these things seemed pointless. It was all I could do to get out of bed in the morning. I decided my work was a crock. I decided that people shouldn't have kids at all— there's too much pain involved. Someone, sensing my downward spiral, gave me the book *Don't Sweat the Small Stuff . . . And It's All Small Stuff.* My suicidal fantasies morphed into homicidal urges. Because, I'm sorry, but sometimes it's really big stuff. One afternoon at a neighborhood park, looking around at the other mothers, I had the urge to tell them they were naive and selfish, that they could only promise their children suffering.

I tried to shop for "court clothes" and hair dye that would make me look, as my daughter started calling the style I was going for, "not-punk." But the Clairol dye I chose just turned my hair from pink to emerald green, and the high-heeled shoes I tried on at Payless ShoeSource pressed against the sides of my feet so uncomfortably, they made me think fondly of death.

When my attorney withdrew from the case and I had to hire another, I just shook my head as I handed over the fifteen hundred dollars I'd set aside for Maia's school bill.

When an unexpected letter came from the Department of Motor Vehicles informing me that because I had turned in my signed-off fix-it ticket for a burnt-out taillight a day too late, my right to operate a motor vehicle was suspended, it didn't even occur to me to pick up the phone to yell at someone. I just sighed and took the notice as yet another sign that the universe was a merciless place.

A friend chirped, "You create your own reality." I promptly removed her from my reality and didn't speak to her again for eight months.

Maia actually started complaining: "I cannot eat another Happy Meal."

I scanned my aromatherapy oils, my CD collection and the small bookshelf next to my bed for an elixir, but found none. How many self-help/spiritual/"all is well" books can a girl read? How many afternoons of Oprah? I unplugged the phone. I stopped answering the door. I decided that my state of mind had nothing to do with family court and everything to do with age and destiny. I decided that whatever fire had once burned in me had been extinguished; there wasn't even a spark left to fan.

One morning when I thought it was all I could do to get up, I pulled myself out of bed, walked into the kitchen and scanned the cupboard for a clean coffee mug. There wasn't one. I walked over and stared for a long time at the mountain of dirty dishes in the sink. I just knew I'd never be able to wash them all.

It hadn't rained in the night, but by the damp smell coming in through the window over the sink, I could tell that the dull California winter was finally coming on. And because driving onto the Bay Bridge and hurling myself off the edge seemed like way too big an effort, I decided to do one dish. And then another. I washed spaghetti sauce off the four *Hercules* plates we got from McDonald's. I scrubbed and rinsed every coffee cup I own. I threw away all the leftover soggy cereal in the bowls. I washed the pots, the utensils, the colander full of old, dried-out pasta. I rinsed each dish and set it on the rack to dry. Then, as I had learned to do in seventh-grade home economics, I washed the sink itself and wiped it dry.

Somehow then, for a split second, looking at that spotless sink, I knew—I knew for certain—that it would not be so very long before the world seemed beautiful to me again.

I am not telling you all this because I have some magical cure to offer you. My depression lasted a long time. I am telling you this because if this season has been the same for you, then I want you to know that you are not alone. And if you think it will never let up, well, I want you to know that you are probably mistaken. It will let up, slowly. It will let up whether you ask it to or not. And if you wake up one dull morning and feel as if it's all you can do to get out of bed, just get out of bed.

My Blue Period

When the moon waxes full twice in one month, the second full moon is called a "blue moon." I once got my period twice in one month. Shall we call it my "blue period"?

Women are twice as likely as men to become depressed. And women with children, more likely still. Motherhood breaks our hearts. Depression can sneak in like a cat burglar, making us feel sad and empty. Sometimes it's not that we don't want to get out of bed in the morning. It's that we honestly feel we can't. We are slowed down, bummed out. We feel as though we're lost in a murky wood, worthless and guilty. We try to sleep, but we are filled with self-loathing. We get up to start work on a tragedy in blank verse, but we can't concentrate. Our children see us crying and ask what's wrong. Their concern only makes us sadder.

Biology and hormones can play a part in our tendency toward depression. Two-thirds of women experience some degree of postpartum "blues." Many experience mild to serious depression in the early years of motherhood. In traditional Chinese medicine, women are treated for three years after giving birth to restore hormonal balance. Our predisposition to depression may also have to do with societal roles, lack of privacy, our habitual self-sacrificing, exhaustion and the impossible time binds that result in neglect of our inner lives.

Depression may pass. It almost always does. But it calls on us to reevaluate the way we live. It calls on us to reconnect with ourselves, to reinvent ourselves in our roles as mothers, caring deeply without crumbling under the weight of our cares. Depression calls on us to soften up, to open up, to let it out, to lay down our armor, to take time out, to get real, to find our own way when there is no clear path.

There is no universal formula for curing depression. What ultimately flips the switch and signals a return to well-being is different for each of us. Among the hundreds of mothers I have talked to who have experienced a blue period—ranging from a few days to a few years—the cures are as diverse as the triggers.

The triggers can be physical, emotional, spiritual, environmental and even political imbalances. The physical problems depression can signal include low blood-sugar, thyroid problems and even diseases like syphilis and cancer. If your depression lasts more than a week, it's a good idea to get a full physical exam and rule out serious medical conditions. You may want to look at your diet—too many carbohydrates and not enough tuna melts make me feel panicky and weird. Hormonal imbalances are common culprits, too, and can be addressed by herbalists and traditional Chinese therapies such as acupuncture. The political imbalances caused by war, injustice and environmental degradation can also bring on a sense of hopelessness and depression. Talking and activism are the cures for political depression. Caged animals often show symptoms of clinical depression. Even if we are not literally incarcerated, feeling overdomesticated and trapped by our lives can cause serious depression. Finally, depression is knowledge withheld, intuition withheld. It is knowing what we need to do and pretending we don't know. It is knowing and not being able to act on what we know. It is the endless scrubbing we do when we know perfectly well that there is no such thing as whiter than white.

Diet, exercise and herbal boosters alone aren't likely to pull you out of a serious depression, but staying physically healthy and taking care of yourself will set the stage for whatever it is that ultimately flips the switch.

The worst thing about being depressed is that it feels as if the fog will never lift. But it will. Know that it will. Keep talking. Keep getting out of bed. Do your work. Take time to sit alone with your depression. It may have something to teach you. Rent *American Beauty* and *Without You I'm Nothing* on video. Get out there and fight the good fight, whether you feel like it or not. "It's no use," the part of you that thrives on the safety of your depression will tell you. But it is of great use. Nurture your soul-life, even if it seems hopeless.

In my own life, I have found no better remedy for depression than activism coupled with time to myself. It's not an instant cure by any means, but I have found it more effective than sixty tablets of Wellbutrin. It was no coincidence that my own bout with depression coincided with my battle in family court. And maybe the case wouldn't have gone on for so long if I'd had my spirits about me, but the slender thread of hope at the heart of my nearly overwhelming cynicism saved my ass. Find that slender thread. It will save your ass, too.

Room in The Dark, Part Two

KOKO

I've been going through a few months now when two to four days per week I feel very low-energy and sad. I have friends who have been through real depressions, and I know this is not that—it's not that bad. I'm working with a counselor, and when I see her I work on some really deep stuff and often leave feeling great for the rest of the day but by the next day I crash. I'm having to focus all my energy on keeping the house picked up and feeding my family. Anything extra feels oppressive. I can't even get myself to fold the laundry today. Even my kids couldn't perk me up today. I'm afraid if this doesn't let up my house will fall apart around me (and make me more depressed!), my kids will watch way too much TV, my family won't have good food to eat and my husband and friends won't want to talk to me anymore. Has anyone out there gone through this?

JANE

I've been there. Facing one's demons—especially your deepest most repressed ones—is the hardest thing you could ever hope to do. Then add to that trying to help

*everyone else, especially kids, and you have quite the
volatile mixture. I've heard that St. John's Wort (or
Mother Wort if you are still nursing) helps quite a bit, but
when I'm in the thick of ickiness it never occurs to me. It's
also a cumulative thing so you have to have a shred of
motivation—which is very hard to find when you're
depressed. The only advice I can offer is to keep talking.
Tell the counselor about the inevitable crash.*

VERA

*I have a history of depression—was even hospitalized for
it when I was seventeen. I know what you mean. For the
past not-sure-how-long I've been feeling that way—not
even being able to do the things you still are able to—pick
up house, laundry. My husband has been carrying the
brunt of the load and doing most of the day-to-day caring
for our daughter. I recently decided it was getting bad
enough that I went back on an antidepressant. I think it's
helping. I truly believe what would help you and me both
the most would be to get regular exercise—any increase in
activity level would help. And a short, daily dose of
sunlight. But most of the time I cannot get myself up and
out to do something. As much as I know how much
better I would feel if I would "just do it"—I just can't. For
me, it helped to be validated, when my doctor actually
diagnosed me with "depression"—made me feel better just
knowing that I'm not simply lazy. There is so much that
I want to do—and because I, like you, am recognizing the
early signs, we can take measures to prevent a major
episode of depression that could possibly render us*

literally dysfunctional. I don't ever want to go back to that, I don't think anyone does.

JULIA

I've been there, too. I haven't had to go as far as getting any meds, but sometimes I wonder what it would be like if I did actually use them. One of the things I have been afraid of is appearing weak. It sucks. I know how hard it is. I have noticed that when I go through the funk, I am much, much better afterwards than I was before. I am stronger and more clear on my beliefs and goals and feelings. It's weird. I don't recommend just waiting it out. If it helps to set small goals for yourself so you feel like you accomplished something for yourself, by all means do it. Also, give yourself permission to not have to do anything if that's what you want.

SIERRA

Aaaah, I saw a T-shirt recently that I think is thera-peutic all by itself; it says "Next Mood Swing in Only Six Minutes!" Of course, there are times when I wouldn't think that was funny at all. Take a look at your diet; stuff like sugar, caffeine and alcohol (even a little bit if you're sensitive to it) can make that kind of roller coaster shit worse. Keep talking to your counse-lor, but also try to get at the problem from another direction—the diet thing, meditation, yoga, tai chi or even chiropractic if you find the right chiropractor. I also recommend spending time sitting under a tree blowing soap bubbles.

JAZZ

*Or flying a kite. Sometimes just turning off that damn TV
can make such a difference. That box can suck everything out of you. Hang in there, and take these smart
mamas' advice.*

KATE

*I have been down very similar roads in my life, so you
are not alone. I would advise strongly against pushing
yourself. People who say that have no clue and should be
ignored. The only thing that has ever truly worked for me
(in combination with therapy and meds) is to cut back to
the bare essentials. Then I slowly add activities as I can
handle them. I am actually in a "cutting down" cycle
right now because I could feel the depression creeping
back in. I'm proud that I am learning to listen to my body
and soul. It sounds like you are learning to do the same
thing, and that is really the key. Best wishes.*

Six Depression Dreams

I.   I go into a museum and see a small rock sculpture my mother made for me when I was a kid. I know it is the same one because it has her initials on it, but I leave it in the museum.

II.   I go to my mother's house. It is twice its original size. Most of the rooms are empty, and my mother wants to know if she should keep the windows open at night. I tell her "yes" and ask where all the furniture has gone. "All sold," she tells me. "All sold for much less than it was worth."

III.   I take the stand in family court and swear to tell the truth, but the questions are all a mumble. I notice a small fire in the back of the courtroom, but all eyes are on me. I gesture toward the door, "We have to get out." But they do not see. The fire spreads, traps us all. And they are still waiting for the whole truth.

IV.   The people doing the custody evaluation make me take the Minnesota Multiphasic Personality Inventory over and over again because I answer too many of the questions "true."

V. I arrive in court late, and my case is already being heard. Some lawyers are reading my astrological chart and arguing that mothers should not be Cancer, Scorpio rising. I stand at the back of the courtroom, hoping they won't notice me, shooting poisoned arrows at their backs.

VI. I am in the Pacific Ocean, and I notice a sign: Swim At Your Own Risk. An undertow pulls me out past the horizon. I am falling in black space.

Jeff Calls to Cheer Me Up

*It's us versus them, the artists versus the drones, and
there are thirty thousand drones for every artist. But
we will be victorious.*

JEFF

About six months into my increasingly annoying depression,
my friend Jeff called to see how I was doing. I didn't waste
any time with "pretty good's." I felt like shit, I told him, and
had for a long time. I was getting tired of it. "I don't mind
feeling bad for a few weeks at a time," I said. "I can handle
the ebb and flow thing. But this—this is beginning to feel like
a *period of my life*, you know?"

"Yeah," he said. "Everyone I've talked to lately is either
doing really well or really badly. There doesn't seem to be
much in-between going around."

I immediately suggested that we shoot all the people
who were doing "really well." And even though my idea
struck Jeff as a novel solution, he had to object. "No," he told
me. "I'm one of the people doing really well. I feel great!"

I hadn't realized.

He started helping me brainstorm ways to get out of my funk. Getting laid was, quite characteristically, at the top of his list. Next came exercise. "It sounds cheesy," Jeff told me. "But your body is simple. If you get out and exercise, if you really get your body pumped, your body can't be unhappy, and then it can start to fool your mind into thinking that the world isn't such a crappy place, which of course it is."

This sounded all right, but I complained that I didn't have the energy to exercise.

Pretty soon Jeff gave up trying to cheer me up. His dad had come to see him recently, so he decided to tell me about that instead. His dad is one of those people who, as Jeff puts it, "doesn't know about anything but Wall Street." Father and son agreed over wine that the country was going to hell, but problem number one, according to Dad, was the moral decline among the likes of Jeff and myself—our "anything goes" attitude that is all too prevalent in the San Francisco Bay Area.

Jeff went on to tell me that he was recovering from "the mother of all hangovers" because of his birthday party the night before, that he hadn't had sex in three weeks and wasn't going to be able to go on much longer, that he'd spent two years with his ex-boyfriend and felt nothing upon their breakup, that he couldn't stand rap music and his neighbor blared it twenty-four hours a day, and that he thought we had until about the year 2010 to live under the illusion of freedom, after which our government would be replaced by an honest tyranny.

At this point in the conversation I remembered that Jeff had started out by telling me he was doing "really well."

"We are just specks of dust on the swelling abscess that is America . . . " he was saying.

"Well," I finally interrupted. "It's great to hear what people think about when they're not depressed."

And we laughed, both feeling strangely liberated by how similar "really well" and "really badly" can be.

My Country 'Tis of Thee

Fighting for peace is like fucking for virginity.

1960s antiwar slogan

As I write this, the president is on television feigning shock at the latest reports of school violence. He's urging our nation's kids to "resolve their conflicts with words, not weapons." After a commercial break—in which I learn the special enzymes in a new laundry detergent will make my linens whiter than white—the headline news cuts to U.S. bombs pounding Yugoslavia. Words, not weapons. Twenty-four more "Apache" helicopters have been deployed to the region, allegedly to protest ethnic cleansing. Later in the broadcast I am introduced to a black Vietnam vet who was awarded a purple heart for bravery while on death row at San Quentin. He has a week to live.

By the time you read this, the names of the countries we have not officially declared war on may have changed. The names of the president and the world leader currently doing CNN's good guy/bad guy routine may have changed. Perhaps some scientific breakthrough will have given us a miraculous chemical compound that makes our sheets and clothes completely disappear. A sort of lethal injection for laundry.

In any case, I have a sinking premonition that despite any name changes or scientific breakthroughs, the television news will still be full of a bunch of old white guys fighting for peace, interrupted by a bunch of white chicks who can't seem to get the blood out of their loved ones' clothes. The war hero will have been killed, and I'll still be here at home fucking for virginity on not-so-white sheets and singing "My Country 'Tis of Thee."

Please tell me: *There will be child care at the revolution.*

Sixty Tablets of Wellbutrin
(May Cause Drowsiness)

I went up to Bellingham, Washington, to talk with some mamas recently. One woman told me that when her food stamps were cut off, she gave up plans to go to college and went to work full-time. She'd wake up crying after dreams of taking her baby to the park. She went to the counseling center for help, and they put her on an antidepressant. The side effects were worse than the breakdown. They adjusted the dose, then the drug, then the dose again until finally she cheered up. She still dreamed of going back to school and taking her kid to the park, but she didn't care so much about not doing those things.

The U.S. government saved $1.3 billion by raiding your food stamps in 1999. The cash came in handy, paying for the first few days of bombing Yugoslavia.

Who needs to eat—or go to the park—in a free country?

Another mom got a day job and a night job. She went to a local service center for help and they offered to help her find nighttime daycare. That will help her productivity, but, honestly, do we really need our mothers working day jobs *and* night jobs?

Maybe her next stop will be the counseling center.

No use changing the world, after all, when we can just change everyone's brain chemistry.

I took an antidepressant for a few weeks last winter. It made me crabby and paranoid. I paced the hall for hours, and all the muscles in my back felt like rocks. I called the doctor to complain, but he advised me to keep taking the medication. He told me: If it doesn't alter your mood, at least it will make you lose weight.

Marvelous. I'm sure my butt size is my real problem.

I felt so fabulous when I finally stopped taking the drug that I wondered if maybe that wasn't the trick: Give me a taste of how bad I could really feel, and I'd come to appreciate my own natural, relatively mild angst.

I know the drugs work for some folks. One in two, according to the statistics. Placebos work on only one in three. Research money is being poured into the study of brain chemistry and the development of these drugs even as mental health coverage is cut and cut and cut.

Now, I don't hold anybody's meds against them. If you've found that they're the only thing that gets you up in the morning, I understand. Believe me. But please remember: They may make you politically cooperative. So, you might have to get pretty conscious and deliberate about not going along with this nonsense once you do get up. Meds or no— keep telling the truth, even when it seems impossible to tell. Keep taking care of yourself, even when you're feeling "just fine!" Go to the park. And keep raising hell, because we all deserve a humane world where we can survive and thrive— even with our own funky little brain chemistries.

A Return to Rage

Living in the whitey Zen culture of the San Francisco Bay Area, you hear a lot of talk about loving-kindness. As mothers, our empathy for others is naturally heightened. We teach our children to resolve conflicts peacefully. And we learn to see the child in everyone. This can be awesome. It softens us. But be careful. There *are* people in this world whose actions are not worthy of our tolerance or our loving-kindness. A lot of assholes are running around out there. Learn to discriminate.

Do not let loving-kindness become your excuse for apathy. As women, and as mothers, we are already socialized to be doormats. It's important to be kind, yes. And loving, yes, yes. It's important to give people the benefit of the doubt. But it is important, also, to be fierce, to be firm when that's called for. I read recently that people who complain live longer. ("Of course," says Susan Jane Gilman, "there's always the possibility that this is because the people who have to listen to them die sooner, but who's to say?") I know too many good women who swallow their frustration, who shrug off fighting the good fight, who don't bother to stand up for themselves and their families, who become doormats in the name of some hokey New Age peace and love thing, who try to communicate, to talk things out with assholes and predators. I know too many good women who have accepted oppression as their karma. That acceptance only causes worse karma. It causes depression and tumors, too.

The late socialist-feminist Clara Fraser said it best: "Love your enemy—love, love, love, love, love. Barf."

When we are needlessly argumentative, overly defensive or judgmental, it's a good idea to work on becoming more accepting of this world and the people who roam it. But when we see injustice, we have to stand and testify. When we are attacked, we have to fight back.

Recently, a serial rapist was terrorizing my Oakland neighborhood. Police flyers appeared on telephone poles and in cafe windows. "Women Beware," the flyers read. "There is a rapist in this neighborhood . . . "

The women on my block could have locked themselves in their homes and sent healing thoughts to this asshole. We could have concerned ourselves with the probability that he, too, had been wounded. We could have accepted our "karma" and hoped that destiny, or the cops, would take care of the problem. Instead, the women in my neighborhood put up a few flyers of our own: "Rapist Beware," they read. "There are women in this neighborhood who will cut your dick off . . . " And I like to think we would have. But we did not hear from him again.

There is a time for loving-kindness, a time for empathy and karma, and there is a time to complain, a time to kick ass. Don't forget that.

Putting the "Fun" Back
in "Dysfunctional"

Instant gratification takes too long.

CARRIE FISHER

I'm sitting at my kitchen table reading a sort of anti-Jazzercise/
anti-calming down treatise in *HUES* magazine. The author,
Susan Jane Gilman, claims the real antidote for whatever
ails heart and soul isn't deep breathing or candle lighting—
it's a trip to Las Vegas. And I think she's quite serious.

> *In Las Vegas, nobody cares how much you weigh.*
> *Nobody cares how you dress. Nobody cares what you*
> *look like, how stylish you are, how sexy you are, or*
> *whether you speak English. As long as you can afford the*
> *$4.99 all-you-can-eat buffet plus a few quarters for the*
> *slot machines, the Vegas folks are thrilled to wait on you*
> *hand and foot. . . . Equally important, Vegas is cheap.*
> *And it's a city that wants you to relax and indulge*
> *yourself. Nobody's waking you up at 6:00 A.M. to go on a*
> *sixteen-mile nature walk. You can stay up all night, chow*
> *down on pancakes and prime rib twenty-four hours a*

*day, wear gaudy clothing and comfortable shoes, ride
from casino to casino in a trolley, dance, scream, laugh,
and flirt, and nobody will encourage you to do otherwise.*

Wow. Who knew? Well, okay, a few people. It's only the
second most popular tourist destination in the United States
(after Disney World, Orlando, of course). I've never thought
of Vegas as quite my speed, but here Gilman insists that the
cheesy vacation spot is "better for the heart and soul than
anything in a vicious little gymnasium."

Thirty million visitors a year can't be wrong, can they?
Let's jump in the Honda and find out!

A quick glance at the hotel brochure on the way, and I understand we're in for a full-calamity vacation: Circus Circus is a
casino, hotel, resort, spa, five-acre Grand Canyon Slam
theme park, year-round circus and wedding chapel all in
one. Thirty-five bucks a night gets us a room in the West
Tower with a view of the bungee-jumpers and a couple of
lunch buffets. I quickly learn, too, that the Mojave Desert is
wider and hotter than it looks on the map.

No matter. I'm wearing a bright rose-patterned polyes-
ter mini-dress, and my hair, which has taken on a strange
iridescent green glow after too many kitchen-sink dyeing
disasters, is in Pippi Longstocking braids. My Honda's got air
conditioning, and I'm driving with my girlfriend Karen, Maia
and Maia's friend Maddi. I figure we'll either have a blast or
the seventy-two-hour catastrophe will make my hectic
home-life feel like a stroll in the park at dusk.

❖

About half the people we had mentioned our destination to before we left had looked at us in horror. "Why?" The other half had laughed and told us we'd have great fun. As it turned out, the "great fun" people were right, but it's easy to see why the city inspires just as many looks of horror.

Three days was the perfect length of stay. Long enough to win a hundred dollars in quarters and watch the kids spend it all on arcade games, but not long enough to get fixated on the idea that we were on the verge of a really big jackpot and should spend our life savings getting to it. Three days was long enough to let the overstimulation of casinos, theme parks, circuses, cable TVs and gluttonous buffet crowds drown out any problems that may have been weighing on our minds, but not long enough to let this new madness creep in. Three days was long enough to walk around with our mouths hanging open, marveling at the strange and chaotic culture we call our own, but not long enough to start deconstructing it and ultimately opt for a full frontal lobotomy.

If you've been to Vegas before, you know what I'm talking about. But if you haven't had the bizarre pleasure, you must check it out.

How Unromantic Is That?

Children of the future Age,
Reading this indignant page;
Know that in a former time.
Love! sweet Love! was thought a crime.
                    WILLIAM BLAKE, *Songs of Experience*

Having a baby can dull the sex drive for a while. The hormones. The exhaustion. The time of no time. It's natural. It can be our body's way of saying, *um, one baby is enough for the time being, thank you very much*. But lust returns. A day or a month or a year and suddenly you feel like your pre-mama self again. Or do you? Your sex drive may be back in full force, but gone are the days of a leisurely morning of making love. Now you have to schedule your sex life. *How unromantic is that?* you think to yourself. Gone are the days of late-night screams. Now it's mostly muffled gasps. You bite your lover's shoulder. It's like being in a college dorm room again, only now you're listening for the patter of little feet.

My sister called me one day when her son was four or five. She was ranting about some woman who had given her a complicated herbal recipe to make the perfect masturbation bath. "Who has time for this?" She was practically screaming into the phone. "Who?"

"Sounds like maybe you better *make* time," I joked. But, of course, I wasn't really kidding.

Lack of sex is bad for the brain, bad for the spirit, bad for the relationship—if there is one—and bad for the heart. If you have sex with yourself mostly, you'll find you can get off here and there—an hour in the bathtub after the children have gone to bed, twenty minutes in the morning before they get up, in the car between daycare drop-off and work. But if you have a husband or lover, you have to put aside that first *How unromantic is that?* reaction and get out the day planner. The predictable strains parenthood puts on your relationship are severe enough without adding major bouts of frustration to the list. You need hours alone. You need a baby sitter. You need romantic getaways.

My friend and her partner were fortunate to have all of the above. When their baby was four months old, another couple took her for the weekend and my friend and her partner reserved a hotel room for their getaway. The sitters brought the baby in to nurse, but the rest of the time my friend and her partner slept in, ordered room service, took hot baths and made love without listening for anyone at all.

Become a Morning Person

I am not naturally a morning person. But when I was small and both my sister and my mother had already settled into their roles of night people, I used to set my clock radio for 5:00 A.M. and get up—when I could—to wander down our long hallway, stand over the heater vent in the living room, and watch the dust dance in the perfect ray of morning light that shone in through a tiny arched window in our front door.

I would stand as quietly as I could, watching the light and listening to the loud *tick tock* of the grandfather clock, and wait for my stepfather to notice me. He was half-deaf and usually deep in concentration—writing a sermon for his Sunday Mass, jotting down notes in his diary or just gazing out the living room window, sipping a mug full of hot water and eating a bowl of dry granola covered with honey. Still, I felt a great sense of accomplishment on the mornings I could stand silently for a full hour before he saw me. By then it would be time to go into the kitchen for breakfast. My stepfather and I would sit on the funny stools he had padded with rust-colored carpet remnants and talk about God, make fun of each other's tastes in breakfast foods and wait for my mother and sister to come stumbling in, complaining about the injustice of a sound sleep interrupted.

Sylvia Plath, who wrote her most haunting and personal poetry after her children were born, got up every morning at four during the last few months of her life. There was never time and self except in that "still blue almost eternal hour before the baby's cry." It was during those hours that she wrote *Ariel*, a book I picked up when I was very young because of its title, but came to cherish only after I became a mother.

Mothers of newborns are often advised to "sleep when the baby sleeps." And this is certainly better than catching up on work or taking out the garbage while the baby sleeps. But often it's not just sleep we need—we need quiet. More time and self. That "still blue almost eternal hour" to write or to paint or to watch the dust dance in the sunlight or to sip hot water and watch out the window as the squirrels and the blue jays begin to make their morning rounds.

Time of No Time

*Make a break for it—flee out into the wilderness—the one
within if you can find it.*

UTAH PHILLIPS, "Natural Resources"

"Not wanting to parent full-time" was the topic du jour on
hipmama.com. "Give me joint custody, hold the divorce!"
one mother insisted. As soon as she'd let this cat out of the
bag, dozens of women chimed in with their secret wishes for
time to themselves.

"But who can do the job as well as I can?" one mother
asked, second-guessing her own desire for some time off.

"I'd say that on days when I'm crabby, impatient, exhausted and irritable, almost anyone can do the job as well,
even better," another mama reminded us. "I don't do my kids
justice when I'm burnt out."

The basic commitment I want you to make right now is
to take time out for yourself. I know this is a good deal to ask.
"Time is money," someone screamed at me on the phone
this morning. Time is not money. But time has become a
precious commodity. We have twenty-four hours in each
day, seven days in each week. We have some hundred years

on this earth. We can think of time as linear or cyclical. Either way, we can't get enough of it. "Where does the time go?" These words were scribbled on a postcard that appeared in my post office box last week. "Or does it exist at all?"

In a recent *Parenting* magazine survey, women cited lack of time with our children as the greatest obstacle to being better mothers. (The second greatest obstacle was lack of money.) If we can squeeze an extra hour out of our hectic schedules, our instinct is to give that time to our children. This is not a bad instinct. But we also need time for ourselves. Some of us are handed our self-time, rather unceremoniously, by a judge. It is called visitation. Or it is called joint custody (a strange practice that has its conceptual roots, I suppose, in the myth of Demeter, Hades and Persephone). The rest of us have to draft our own orders.

I don't think it matters exactly how much time you take, but it is best if it is regular. The stressed body craves its own routine. As little as an hour at dawn and a full week each year has worked for me.

Andrea, a mother of one, writes:

Don't you just love days to yourself? For me it is so overwhelming because I just want to pack in everything all at once. My husband and I each have one designated day a week. On his day, which is Tuesday (after work), he goes into the garage and does his woodworking. On my day, I usually end up going to the bookstore and burying myself in all different kinds of books. I also like to write in my journal. It's nice to be able to find some

time when I'm really not tired. My baby is just about one.
Now I'm aware of how much I took for granted when I
was childless—all the things that I should have done
when I had the time that I would love to do now.

At first you may discover all kinds of resistance to this self-time. You will spend your entire evening out in the city thinking of your children and imagining they need you. Or you will pass the afternoon worrying, pacing the length of your hallway, not knowing quite what to do with yourself. If your time off is court-ordered, you will sit silently on a hard wooden chair next to your phone as all your resentment stews inside. But those feelings will settle down. To rewrite the script we have been handed as mothers, a script of self-sacrifice and damaging stereotypes, we have to take some time to feel our attachment to that script. The alternative is to live with increasing resentment, perpetual PMS, chronic fatigue and depression.

When I first left Maia for an extended visit with her father, it was not of my own free will. Almost nothing about the "parenting plan" that was forced on my family by the Superior Court of California was good for any of its members. But there was this time. This time to myself. And I will always be thankful for that. My time spent in solitude or childless playing was at first restless and painful, but it was in those hours that I found the spirit to rewrite my life script and, in that process, became emboldened to try and rewrite our cultural scripts. It was in those hours that I learned to center on myself and refuel before another hectic week. And it was in those hours that I grew up.

I planned to write this book in the hours when Maia was off with her father. But fate intervened. After five years of mandated visitation, the power of our court order evaporated, along with Maia's father's presence in our lives. It took me some time to adjust. I had to willfully schedule my time to myself, as well as much of my work time, into our family life. I met that old resistance again. But I knew better than to bend to it.

Shared custody or no, I am asking you to make this basic commitment: to save for yourself a small piece of our most precious commodity in this time of no time. I know it is a good deal to ask. I wouldn't ask it if I didn't think your life depended on it. I think it does.

In My Sister's Kitchen

Modern science has recently caught up with my sister, Leslie, and with medicine women and grandmothers from time immemorial. Scientists have "discovered" (surprise!) that chicken vegetable soup contains the perfect electrolyte mineral balance to warm you up and keep you well. If you find that depression has you gobbling down anything you can get your hands on, take time out to make yourself some healthful foods that will actually pick you up.

Vegetables and herbs all have traditional medicinal uses: Carrots are high in vitamin A, which fortifies the immune system; celery is a diuretic and good for bronchitis; onions are a natural blood purifier, as are leeks. Sage, rosemary, thyme, coriander and bay—all mild expectorants and digestives—taste great in soups. Barley water is nutritious and can sooth an irritated stomach. And most green vegetables are high in iron.

All that said, my sister's Medicine Woman Soup is not only good for you, it's a tasty treat.

MEDICINE WOMAN SOUP

Pour three tablespoons of olive oil into a big heavy-bottomed soup pot. Chop up a big leek or onion and some chicken parts (neck, back and innards are fine), and cook them in the pot until the onion is transparent and the chicken is lightly browned (vegetarians: Leave the chicken out, but be sure to add a few extra green things and some tofu). If you've got any dried herbs (bay, rosemary, sage or thyme), add a teaspoon of each at this point. Reduce heat.

Chop up a stalk or two of celery, two carrots, a goodly number of mushrooms, zucchini or whatever vegetables you have in your garden or fridge. Put all these into the pot and add water to a level of two inches over the solid mixture. Toss in a handful of barley, a dash of soy sauce, salt and pepper as you like, and a bouquet made of large sprigs of bay laurel, sage, thyme, rosemary and cilantro.

Cover and cook over medium heat for an hour. You can add some powdered coriander and celery seeds.

Now remove the bouquet, the bones and the icky chicken bits, and serve it up. Don't forget to save your leftovers—the soup will be all the better tomorrow.

CHEER-UP YOGURT

If it's bad digestion that's making you sad or tired, try some cold yogurt soup. Yogurt has enzymes that clean out your intestines, the cucumbers can calm inflamed tissue, and the raw garlic is a natural antibiotic. Together, those ingredients should clean out your system and wake you up.

Combine equal parts plain yogurt and minced cucumber, and add a mashed clove of garlic. Let the mixture sit in

*the fridge for a couple of hours, and then either blend it
in a food processor or eat it chunky.*

CALMING SOUP
Leek and potato soup is good for anemia and anxiety. It's a
diuretic and antiseptic, and it will calm your tummy.

*Chop up equal parts of leeks and potatoes. Put them in
your pot and cover with water. Bring to a boil; then lower
the heat and cook, covered, for about half an hour or
until your potatoes are falling apart. Blend the whole
thing in a food processor until creamy. Add milk or
cream to taste, and garnish with chives or parsley. You
can eat your soup hot, warm or cold.*

SOUND SLEEP DINNER
If you have trouble falling asleep, try eating a turkey burger
with melted cheese and sautéed onions for dinner. The tryp-
tophan in the turkey, onions and cheese will make you
sleepy. Follow this with a glass of warm milk and honey. At
bedtime, put a few drops of essence of chamomile oil on
your pillow. You'll be ready to crash.

PUMPKIN MUFFINS
Ana June just sent me the following e-mail message:

*My son is in the kitchen "washing dishes," my daughter is
nursing back to a sleep I interrupted when I turned on a
blender full of pumpkin muffin mix—the raisins
screamed to high heaven. It's 11:30. We're wasting water*

(in the sink where my son is playing), and I'm feeling on the edge of myself. How to give when I have nothing to give? I want to move far, far away. I wish I wasn't home all the time. Being a stay-at-home mom can be so isolating—I wish I could afford a sitter a few times a week. I am rambling, I am tired. I want so much in this life— right now I just want baked pumpkin muffins and a warm bed.

Preheat your oven to four hundred degrees. Grease a twelve-cup muffin pan. Stir together one and a half cups flour, three-quarters teaspoon salt, a half-cup of sugar, two teaspoons of cinnamon, a half-teaspoon of allspice, a teaspoon of powdered ginger, two teaspoons of grated orange rind, a teaspoon of nutmeg and two teaspoons of baking powder. In another bowl, beat two eggs. To the eggs add three tablespoons of melted butter, a cup of cooked, puréed pumpkin or a cup of canned pumpkin, and three-quarters cup low-fat milk. Combine your wet and dry ingredients and stir just enough to moisten dry ingredients. Fill your muffin pans about two-thirds full and bake twenty to twenty-five minutes.

Eat

When I was a teenager I suffered from the typical Western adolescent's messed-up relationship with food. I threw myself on every new diet that appeared in *Mademoiselle*. I took appetite suppressants and smoked Camel filters to quiet my hunger. I kept my index fingernail clipped short so that I could make myself vomit without scratching my throat. I taught my sister and my best friend, Sid, to do the same. I memorized the food calorie table at the front of *The Joy of Cooking* and could calculate, on sight, the caloric cost of any meal. At the time I thought I would like to be anorexic—if only I could muster the will power. I told myself that never allowing my weight to creep up over one hundred pounds made me feel close to the bone. I was studying Buddhism, too, and sometimes convinced myself I was fasting on a spiritual quest.

One afternoon during my freshman year in high school, Sid and I sat at her kitchen table sharing a bowl of plain white rice and planning our menus for the upcoming week. "One hard-boiled egg for breakfast," we wrote in a spiral notebook. "One piece of fruit for lunch. One bowl of rice for dinner." As if we wouldn't be able to remember our three hundred allotted calories without writing them down.

"It will be so cool when we get pregnant," Sid said dreamily as we decided our diets would begin the next day, and it would be therefore permissible for us to have some fried chicken and chocolate at this point. "Then we can eat whatever we want."

"I'm gonna get so fat when I'm pregnant," I vowed.

This conversation didn't seem the least bit odd to me at the time. We were learning how to be women, taking our cues from the mainstream marketing culture.

It seemed logical to us that if we got pregnant, we would be feeding another (more important) human being. We could feed ourselves then, for the sake of our child.

By the time I got pregnant a few years later, I had already given up on most of my diets. Only the smoking habit held. But I could still calculate, on sight, the caloric cost of any meal. I still saw my body as round and imperfect. But now when I threw up, it was from morning sickness, not purging. Contrary to the vow I'd made that afternoon in Sid's kitchen, I didn't get particularly fat while I was pregnant, but I did finally learn how to eat. I was perpetually broke, so I began to see calories as valuable, rather than costly. I had a tenant in my womb, so I learned to see the brink of starvation as dangerous, rather than desirable.

In the postnatal magazines American marketers showered me with when I came back to the States after Maia was born, I read about all the diets and exercise programs I could embark on to unlearn all of this. They wanted me to get "back in shape," to resculpt my body into a hipless, tummy-less, titless unmaternal thing, to carefully measure anything I might give myself now that I couldn't say I was eating for the sake of my child.

But it was too late. The marketers couldn't win me back. I had discovered that eating is good. That food is good. That appetite is good and needn't be suppressed. Now, if you think I mother my daughter, publish and edit a zine, write and live my life on three hundred—or even two thousand—calories a day, I have news for you. I eat bacon and giant Mexican papayas for breakfast. I slather butter on corn, take cream in my coffee and, yes, real raw sugar please. I eat organic tomatoes in late spring, shell pasta with Gorgonzola cheese on June nights, avocados spooned right out of their skins, bagels with cream cheese and lox. I eat ice cream sundaes for lunch sometimes, crème brûlée for dessert. I'll take the sour cream on the home fries, thank you, and fresh baked bread on the side.

My maternal body is bigger than my teenage body was. And sometimes I still envy my size-four girlfriend. But this is what I have: strong legs, a round belly, childbearing hips, a taste for sugar and cream, and a little prayer for those girls we once were, sitting in Sid's kitchen, thinking we were learning how to be women.

Sleep

The mama lion is fierce, no? A bold role model, she is wild and maternal. So how come, in the photos I took one summer in Africa, all the mama lions are fast asleep?

A mother-friend of mine took a night job last year and came over bragging that she'd finally have the best of all worlds. She'd be home with her kids after daycare and school, she could work while they slept, come home and get them ready for their days and crash out while they were at school from nine until one.

I was impressed.

She lasted four and a half months.

Then my friend came down with a wicked chest cold and couldn't lift her head off her pillow for two weeks. She's lucky that's all it was.

In a pinch, and with enough coffee, we can do anything. I know this from experience. But "pinches" can't happen daily. We have human bodies, after all, you and I and my industrious mother-friend. We need to sleep. Some psychologists tell us we should be sleeping from sunset to sunrise.

That's, like, ten hours. You can do pretty well on eight. You can get by every now and again on less. But listen to your body.

The lioness mothers her cubs well. She nurses them. She is a fierce protector, always alert to danger. She hunts to feed her family (save his gorgeous mane, the male is almost useless). But when all has been hunted and all have been fed, the lioness lays down in the shade of an acacia tree and rests for some twenty-four hours.

Tell Your Secrets

Get together with trustworthy moms, and tell your secrets. Talk. Describe what it's like to live now. Voice your unspoken feelings about motherhood, your children, your loves, your life, agreeing that nothing is unspeakable. That might seem scary at first. Many of us were taught that even impure *thoughts* are sinful. If that is true, we are all hell-bound. Each of us has had, we must admit, every possible kind of thought.

In a writing group I was once in, each participant was asked to write for ten minutes describing an event or thought sequence she considered unspeakable. I thought for a few minutes and focused on the one thing I had never told anyone. And then I proceeded to tell it. I described the afternoon in Italy after I brought my daughter home from the hospital. I was sitting with her in front of a crackling fire when the urge to throw her in it, blanket and all, struck me like a demon out of nowhere. I was not conscious of wanting to hurt her. I was not conscious of much. Perhaps I hoped to make her immortal, like the ancient Greek goddesses.

I was shaking as I read the pages to my writing group. The story was, to me, unspeakable, and the memory of it had haunted me for many months. Later, I included the sequence in a fictional story and, finally, as truth in my first book. No mother I have ever shared the story with has been terribly shocked. My experience, it turned out, was commonplace. Still, when that first book was about to be published, I sat down with my daughter on the end of her bed and told her the story so that she would hear it from me in a loving tone rather than hear it being discussed on some radio show or read it herself in the book. As I told her, I imagined I would have to explain myself, assure her that I would never do such a thing, promise that she has always been loved and wanted. I underestimated her. At age eight she already knew, as Muriel Rukeyser has pointed out, "the universe is made up of stories, not atoms." She responded with a tale of her own and told me of an urge she considered impure and a dream in which she acted on that unspeakable urge.

Some secrets are necessary for survival. But most of the secrets we keep are neither necessary nor helpful. In myth and psychology, it is well understood that that which is unspoken *becomes* unspeakable. It grows out of control like a thick-rooted weed that can strangle every perfectly placed plant and flower in a garden.

In consciousness-raising groups of the early 1970s, women gathered and—over tea or wine—told the truth about their lives. The result, of course, was that the world split open. The movement that emerged from those consciousness-raising groups revolutionized virtually every facet of American culture. Mothers have been slow to follow suit. Our perfect-mother myths persist. Silences and taboos around maternal ambivalence, maternal rage and even maternal mad love endure. The roots of those taboos are thick and deep. It is time to pull them up.

❖

I'll never get used to the reality that motherhood is such an isolating experience. There's hardly a more common profession, yet many of us feel completely alone. Our individual homes and our time constraints keep us from one another. And labels—bad mother, good mother, stay-at-home mother, working mother, single mother and the rest—not only encourage guilt and undermine our efforts but also divide us as potential allies.

Women approach me, call me and e-mail me asking for advice on various aspects of mothering, but often isolation is their real ache. Simply listening is the most profound help we can offer each other.

We may consider the choices we have to make for our families to be some of the most daunting and far-reaching decisions we will make in our lifetimes. Because of that, and because of the mother-guilt our culture hands us, we often grow defensive about our choices. But as we learn to stop judging ourselves, we can also practice not judging other mamas. In our years of parenting, we will want to connect with moms who share our child-rearing philosophies. But if we are also open to other possibilities, if we can learn to simply listen, we can begin to remedy the isolation of motherhood. We can see each other through.

On hipmama.com, moms share parenting philosophies and sometimes debate what is best for our children. Because the forum is large and diverse, the debates sometimes generate self-righteous or defensive postings. But when a mother posted anonymously at midnight that she was considering suicide, that she'd sent her children to stay with her mother and had her death plans in place, everyone abandoned their debates and posted healing thoughts. All night, new messages appeared on the board. The original poster was silent, but the other mothers—not knowing whether the woman was still sitting and watching her monitor in the dark—did not give up. By morning I was getting worried phone calls and e-mail messages. Did I know who Anonymous was? Was she still alive? Still online? What could we do now?

Twelve hours later the woman in crisis posted again. She had been there all along, reading the other mothers' posts, thinking, refusing to call a hotline or any of the mothers online who offered their phone numbers, waiting, staying connected to this one forum where she felt comfortable. We knew nothing about this woman's parenting. We knew virtually nothing about her life. But we saw her through. Maybe she is online right now, seeing another mother through.

PART IV

The Whole Mom

Two or three things I know for sure, and one is that I would rather go naked than wear the coat the world has made for me.

DOROTHY ALLISON, *Two or Three Things I Know for Sure*

Out of the Woods

When Maia was younger, I'd sometimes roll my eyes at folks with older kids who warned me to "enjoy it now." I was always waiting for the next stage (it *had* to get easier). I would complain because friends and acquaintances we met on the street would focus on the baby. I felt shadowlike as I faded into the background, being called upon only for clarifying details: "she's teething" or "thirteen-months-one-week-and-two-days."

But it didn't take me long to find comfort there in the background, relieved of the small talk required of single people without kids—talk of weather, romance and "What are you doing these days?"

Now I find myself with a new identity crisis. It presses hardest against my chest when Maia is off with her dad or I myself am away, but it has more to do with a diverging of paths than with anything geographical.

Now if I told you how much I miss being joined at the hip with my daughter, you might roll your eyes. If I admitted that I still calculate, periodically, Maia's precise age, you might let out a little sigh at my sentimentalism. But that's cool. I'm going to tell you about this new identity crisis anyway, because it is an impossibly hot August day and I am riding a New York subway on my way to the airport when it occurs to me as I miss the Jay Street stop that I should carry a pager so that Maia could reach me in an emergency; then, almost simultaneously, it occurs to me that even with the pager I would be totally helpless to act.

So this is my new identity crisis:

It is a free-floating anxiety that attaches itself to telephones that ring too late at night.

It is meeting a woman at a party who asks me how old Maia is. I say "seven," and the woman says "so you're out of the woods," and suddenly I have the urge to correct myself: "seven-and-a-half-and-a-week-and-two-days, actually." Out of the woods.

It is a bath I can steep in, uninterrupted, until the water gets cold.

It is "No, Maia, you cannot borrow my platform shoes."

It is the realization that I have absolutely no adult life experience without being "Mama."

It is listening to friends without kids complain about how weird their moms are and offering, "I can tell you how she got that way."

It is leaning over instinctively to let Maia climb up onto my hip when she is tired and falling over as she lifts her full weight onto my side.

It is no one ever saying "you look too young to be a mother" anymore.

❖

It is an impossibly hot August day on a New York subway, and I miss those crazy woods so much my jaw hurts.

Anchored

> *[B]ecause I am a woman involved in practical concerns, I cannot give the first half of the day to these things, but must meditate when I can, early in the morning and on the fly during the day. Not in the privacy of a study—but here, there and everywhere—at the kitchen table, on the train, on the ferry, on my way to and from appointments and even while making supper or putting Teresa to bed.*
>
> DOROTHY DAY, *Meditations*

When I first read Natalie Goldberg's memoir, *Long Quiet Highway*, at twenty-six, it made me sad.

She described standing in front of a sixth-grade class in Albuquerque—her first regular teaching job—when, without much warning, the Garden of Eden opened in her heart.

Within a week or two Natalie quit the job, gave notice to her landlord, packed up and moved to a commune in northern New Mexico, where she studied under religious teachers from many different traditions and found a meditation practice "to water that garden." She was twenty-six years old.

I put the book down, went out on my balcony and looked up at the starless night sky. Maia was already asleep. What would I do, I wondered, if the Garden of Eden opened in my heart?

I tried to comfort myself with the reality that it hadn't. I could burn that bridge when I got to it. My only adult religious experiences to date could be explained away quite easily as the result of chronic sleep-deprivation. Still, the image of Natalie and the pure freedom of her twenty-sixth year made me sad. Not jealous, exactly. Not even nostalgic. Just sad.

When I was pregnant, everyone from my grandmother to my best high school girlfriends warned me I was too young to give up the autonomy and privilege of life without children. But I hadn't felt the limitation until now. Perhaps being unmarried and having just one preschool-aged child had afforded me the illusion of mobility, of flexibility. But now Maia was in school. Now I was thinking about having a second kid. Now I had lived in the same town for a record five years. Now I was reading *Long Quiet Highway*. And now if the Garden of Eden opened in my heart as I was ordering anchovy pizza and garden salads one bright evening in early spring, well, what could I do but wait for the pizza?

I could tell myself I was still mobile, still flexible. I thought of all the hippie families I grew up with and around. My own parents packed up my sister and me when we were babies to follow my father's art career across Europe. But even the hippies gave up their questing when their children hit school age. By the time my sister was ready for first grade, my mother was single and living in the town where my sister and I would grow up, and where she still lives with my stepfather.

For the first seven years of my daughter's life I was physically, emotionally, spiritually and intellectually all mother. The little knot of relationships I called my family was portable, but still knotlike. Motherhood was all-encompassing.

But now I was experiencing an element of settling. As Maia began to explore the world outside our immediate family, as she settled into school, the neighborhood and friendships, my time binds eased slightly. The knot began to loosen. I returned to my own body. Now my challenges are more intellectual than physical, more practical than emotional. But I feel the anchoring power of my small family.

Some mamas I know have dropped everything one day, quit their jobs and given notice to their landlords because the Garden of Eden has, without much warning, opened in their heart. But if it ever happens to me, I think I will simply take notice, give thanks and wait for the pizza. I am not able to give the first half of the day to these things. And I am learning—slowly, without dramatic change of scenery—to meditate when I can, early in the morning and on the fly during the day. Not in the privacy of a study or a zendo or a church—but here, there and everywhere—at the kitchen table, on the train, on the ferry, on my way to and from appointments and even while making supper or putting Maia to bed.

My Little Atheist

When Maia turned seven, she announced to me that she was an atheist.

"Really?" I said, stunned. "You don't believe in God?"

"Nope."

"Goddess?"

"Nope."

I was heartbroken. I couldn't imagine a life without spirituality. I moped around for a few days. But then I took her new point of view as a maternal challenge. Could I nurture reverence in my kid, could I teach her to honor spirit even if she did not, for the time being, believe in God? Of course I could.

Whether or not you are a religious or faith-observing person, you can always honor spirit. You can leave time for reflection. You can trust life in its intrinsic elegance. You can create a sacred space. You can take a walk. You can make love. You can meditate on the fly, lay down your armor. You can trip on the expanding universe. You can listen to elders, tell stories, say grace. You can make a mess in the garden, nourish your soul-life, be a mama. Spirit doesn't require you to call it by a certain name, believe in a particular text.

Believing in yourself is enough. Believing in your family. And find some space in your busy day to pause and honor it all.

That's what I teach my little atheist, anyway.

Cool-Weird

I am "soooo retro." I dress "like a teenager on Mars." My hair is going to fall out if I keep dyeing it. My work is "just not interesting." I am going to regret getting that last tattoo. Nobody knows how weird I am.

All this according to my daughter and number one style critic, Maia.

I have tried to explain to Maia that, as parents go, I'm really not all that weird. But she doesn't buy it.

I try to remember my own girl-years. My mom was weird. She was small and intense and dressed in what my schoolmates called "Gypsy wear." You know, the early seventies hippie thing with the bandanna, the big gold hoop earrings and the flowing skirt. She had a skeleton named Esmerelda that she dressed in various costumes and propped up around the house. She kept dead birds in the freezer for future art projects.

My dad was weirder. He used to show up outside my elementary school in a Louis XIV wig and play the trumpet. (Okay, so he only did that once, but he'll never live it down.)

My stepfather was the least weird parent in the family, but even he recycled Dixie cups into chandeliers and would occasionally remove his false teeth in the middle of a conversation.

My parents had friends who, in retrospect, were even weirder than they were. One guy used to come over on holidays and invariably ended up in the back yard howling at the moon. Another insisted he was the president of the United States. One used to show up for dinner unannounced and tell us all about the aliens who were coming to take him home "any day now." We waited.

Even so, as a kid, I felt as if my own three parents were as bizarre and embarrassing as it got. Other kids' parents always seemed to have much plainer wardrobes, better-kempt hair and pantries stocked with boxed and canned foods instead of the piles of grains and soy products and dead birds I found at home.

Maia's met some real freaks in her time, too. But none of them appear to rival my weirdness in her mind. Her friends' parents who drive Volvos and shop at The Emporium seem to be her gauge for normalcy.

I have wondered, at times, if I shouldn't try to pull off a more conventional look and lifestyle, for Maia's sake. So, the other morning, when I happened to be wearing a nice pair of navy suit pants and a plain green button-up shirt, I thought she'd be proud to have me walk her into her school. For once in her life she could have a normal mother.

"*Um*, Mom," Maia said as we approached the schoolyard. "Can you just drop me off and go away?"

"Why?" I wanted to know.

"You look, well . . . " she said, trying, apparently, to break it to me gently. "You look positively weird."

"But I look *normal* . . . " I almost whined. "Totally normal."

"Mom," she said, seeming a little exasperated at that point. "My friends think I have a cool-weird mom, okay? Now, if you go up there looking like that, they are going to know you are positively weird. Not cool-weird."

Go figure.

The Tolerance Guy

When Maia and I got home from the San Francisco Gay Pride Parade last summer, there was a message on my voice mail. The father of one of Maia's friends wanted to talk to me about something his daughter had been exposed to on a recent play date at Maia's. Could I call him back?

I didn't know this guy from Adam, but the family lived in a big house, and by the looks of him I figured he was a straight-up Republican. You know the type: white, forty-something, minivan-driving. I dreaded the conversation I could already imagine before me.

Maybe the music on my car stereo had been a bit too anarchistic.

What if he was going to tell me that Maia's *Cow Tse-tung* cartoon was something less than funny?

Maybe his daughter had seen some zine in the study and come home asking what a lesbian was.

Or maybe she'd seen the pro-choice poster in the kitchen and asked what *that* was about.

Whatever it was, surely this kid wasn't going to be allowed to come back to our apartment.

But I called him. I had to.

❖

Me: Hey, it's Ariel—just returning your call.

Him (nervously): Well, when my daughter was over at your house last week . . . well, my wife and I feel she was exposed to something homophobic.

Me (jaw dropping): Homo-what?

Him: Homophobic, anti-gay. It was that video, *Ace Ventura: Pet Detective.*

Me (honestly mortified): Oh, my God. I'm sorry—

Him (more comfortable now): You don't have anything to apologize for. We just wanted to let you know. *Ace Ventura* was featured in *It's Elementary*, the documentary on teaching children tolerance. You know, the documentary will be on PBS next week. You might want to watch it.

Me: Oh. Okay. Thanks. I appreciate your calling.

I'd actually covered the controversy surrounding *It's Elementary* in *Hip Mama*. Apparently I didn't think I needed to watch it myself.

So, thanks again, Tolerance Guy—less for pointing out the homophobic themes in *Ace Ventura* (which is fair enough) than for pointing out the families-who-live-in-big-houses phobia in my head. You never can tell about people.

We Haven't the Haziest

Every once in a while there is a story in the local paper that reminds me why I read the thing at all. This morning the headline that caught my eye announced: "Scientists Find Clues That Universe Is Running Away with Itself."

"There's new evidence," the article began, "from more than a dozen exploding stars in the most distant reaches of space that a mysterious kind of 'antigravity' energy is speeding the expansion of the universe . . . "

It seems that our ever-expanding universe is getting a little carried away with itself, at once defying gravity and conventional scientific wisdom.

What is this strange force that is accelerating starbursts some ten billion light years away? "We haven't the haziest idea," University of California cosmologist Adam Riess told the *San Francisco Chronicle*.

This sublime discovery is, to me, second only to the recent realization by a mathematician tinkering in the far reaches of numeric theory, that arithmetic—simple arithmetic—is not an entirely consistent system within itself. Elegant chaos.

I told my daughter the news about the universe over

breakfast.

Her eyes lit up. "Is it gonna blow?"

"Naah," I told her. "It's just gonna get bigger and bigger and bigger—expanding infinitely in all directions, forever."

For some reason, this thought pleased us both immeasurably, and we went back to eating our Corn Pops with renewed faith that the day ahead would be worthwhile.

Virgins

When the "Sex Matters" department was first added to hipmama.com, folks who visited the site wanted to know our intentions. Were we going to talk about sex education, or were we going to talk about maternal sexuality? As it was, we were going to do both, but this only doubled the number of complaints.

I had always figured sex education was about as controversial a topic as you could tackle, but judging from the responses I've gotten to the Web site and to articles I've run in the *Hip Mama* print zine, the fact that mothers are sexual beings is at least as taboo.

What's up with that? After all, most of us still get pregnant the old-fashioned way, by having sex. And many of us do have more than one kid. So you'd think anyone who'd ever been in a grocery store would have put it together by now. Yes. Mothers have sex. (We also read and think and fart and burp, but I'll save those news flashes for later.)

When I was a new mama living out in the strange suburbs, I was walking across a parking lot toward Kmart one day with my friend Paula. A guy wearing a cowboy hat leaned out his truck window as he passed us, and bellowed,

"Hey, Mom, you need a daddy for that baby?"

"Naw, thanks, already got one too many," I told him.

Paula frowned.

As we approached the sidewalk, a hippie guy passed us and winked, "Hey, sister."

"That's so gross," Paula complained when we got inside the store. And even though I agreed that the guys themselves were sort of gross, I asked her what bugged her about their displays. "You're a mother!" she squealed.

I raised my eyebrows just a little as she stuttered. "I mean, no offense, but, well, you know . . . "

"Because I'm a mother they should be more respectful?"

"Well, no. That's not really what I meant . . . "

I knew what she meant, but I was taking some small sadistic pleasure in watching her squirm.

Maybe it's simpleminded to say the taboo has its roots in the fact that Christians' archetypal mother is said to have been a virgin—and not just before baby Jesus was born, but a virgin for life. Still, I've never gotten as many complaints as when I put the words *mom* and *sex* together on the cover of my zine, and never sold as many copies as when I followed that issue with a cover image of the Virgin Mary.

I won't get into the well-worn arguments about Mary's sexual history, that two thousand years ago, for example, the word we have translated as "virgin" meant only "a woman unto herself." I've lived long enough to know that anything is possible and that miracles are commonplace. But just as the image of Our Lady has been used to encourage us to be self-sacrificing, it has been used to make us feel as if our expressions of sexuality are more base than soulful. And even

Mary was too sexy for the Puritans. In colonial and Victorian America—as in the Bible—women, when we were not totally invisible, could be either virgins or whores. And only the virgins were trusted with the moral upbringing of the kids.

Never mind that everyone over age eight knows that mothers have sex—a lot of folks would just prefer not to think about it. The stork—*yeah*—that's it. We've gotten over some of our sexual taboos in recent decades, but when *mom* and *sex* are mentioned in the same coverline or vaguely suggested by some dorks on the way into Kmart, it's still "Oh, gross."

For that reason, I will always appreciate my grandmother's concerned counsel when Maia was just a few years old. "Do you have a gentleman friend?" she wanted to know.

I ducked the question, presuming I was in for another lecture on the benefits of marriage.

But she persisted. "Because, you know, Ariel, you really need to get some of *that*."

Good Mothers

Most of us know early on all the ways we *don't* want to be like our own parents. And that's cool—we learn from their mistakes. It's evolution. The idealization of moms was no bigger party than the demonization of moms has been. Thinking of our mothers all aglow with white light isn't much more helpful than imagining they were sent from hell with no other assignment than to torture and annoy us. If what we are going for is something more holistic, more real, then we have to continually flip the questions we ask ourselves. Maybe we know the ways we don't want to be like our mothers. But in what ways do we hope to emulate them? What do we want to pass on through the generations?

There's no need for mindless gushing. But do we have innumerable excuses for ourselves and none for the people who raised us?

As we raise our kids, we can't help but see our role in the terms our parents gave us. So I think the way we feel about our first families is worth visiting again and again. As long as they remain idealized or demonized in our heads, there's little hope that we can see ourselves as whole.

I told you about the professionals I met during my struggles in family court—the House Committee on Unmaternal Activities, as my friends and I eventually started referring to them. I told you all the negative things they had to say about my mothering. But they had praise for me, too. Friends who read their reports tried to cheer me up, pointing out all the positive observations the professionals had made about me.

The professionals said I'd created a "nice home" for my family. They said I engaged my daughter in "constructive activities." They mentioned I was a good cook and that I had a "strong support system." They gave me a few brownie points because the subject of my writing is motherhood. They said I'd worked hard to build a life and work schedule around my daughter's needs. I was grateful that the review was not entirely bad. But these positive comments undermined my confidence just as surely as the negative ones did. For the same reason that good reviews of my writing don't actually nurture my work. Good reviews just fatten up my ego for the next guy who wants to sink his teeth in. Praise is kinder than criticism, but it's judgment all the same. It encourages perfectionism, competition, fear, striving and a "this part of me is good"/"that part of me is bad" split. It's as nourishing as sniffing glue.

In an interview with psychologist Harriet Lerner, I called her book *The Mother Dance* one for the "good enough mother." She jumped to correct me, arguing that the phrase "good enough mother" belonged in the judgment pile with the rest of the labels. "Society has always judged and polarized mothers, dividing us into the categories of good mothers and bad mothers," she said. "This false dichotomy belies the fact that if observed over a long enough period of time, most mothers can be both very good and very bad." If what we are moving toward is wholeness rather than perfectionism and a realization and acceptance that we have every aspect in us, then we have to throw out the praise along with the criticism.

I am the honored one and the scorned one.
I am the whore and the holy one.
I am the wife and the virgin.
I am the mother and the daughter . . .
For I am knowledge and ignorance.
I am shame and boldness.
I am shameless; I am ashamed.
I am strength and I am fear . . .
I am the one who has been hated everywhere
and who has been loved everywhere . . .
You honor me . . . and you whisper against me . . .
For I am the one who alone exists,
and I have no one who will judge me.
　　　　　　　Attributed to EVE/LILITH, *The Gnosis Archive*

Bad Press

*You have navigated with raging soul far from the
paternal home, passing beyond the seas' double rocks
and now you inhabit a foreign land.*

—EURIPEDES, *Medea*

I want to tell you about Medea. Yes, the Medea of Greek
tragedy—the mother who did the unthinkable. The one who
killed her own children. The one we despise. And the one
we secretly relate to when we are at our wits' end, about to
collapse under the pressures of work and screaming toddlers
and telephone cut-off notices and Hallmark-card ideals.

But who was Medea, really? She was a priestess of
Hecate, that we know. She was a witch, a midwife. She married Jason, and Jason left her for a princess—the daughter
of the King of Corinth. In her rage over Jason's betrayal,
Medea sent the young princess a deadly wedding gift—a
poisoned robe. The king retaliated, killing thirteen of
Medea's fourteen children and laying their bodies in the
marketplace for all to see.

The king got his revenge, yes, but Corinth's reputation
suffered greatly. Tourism waned. Even four hundred years

later, it seemed no one wanted to visit a country whose king had killed thirteen children. Something had to be done. And so, in the fifth century B.C., Euripides was commissioned to rewrite herstory. In his play, Euripides reduced the number of Medea's children to two and had Medea stab them herself. Corinth's reputation was restored, the king's name cleared and a long journalistic tradition of blaming Mom for all society's failures was born.

Today when we read that a head of state has cut off basic necessities to low-income children, the stories almost always imply the children's predicament was their mothers' fault to begin with. When we read that juvenile crime rates are up, that "children are killing children," the politicians quoted inevitably place the blame squarely on parents. When the economy takes a nose dive, we read awkward sentences in the newspaper designed to convince us that teen pregnancy is somehow to blame. Today the chambers of commerce and the tourism boards and the PR moguls don't wait four hundred years to clear their leaders' names. By now they know the drill. If anything goes wrong in society, *quick, blame Mom.*

So when you read their press releases, when you read the headline "Parents Fail," please remember Medea, and all the others who have been demonized in the media. Remember the welfare mothers, and the teen mothers, and the lesbian mothers, and the single mothers, and the witches, and the midwives, and all the rest of the brave women and maternal feminists who are reinventing family and raising strong children in spite of our bad press. Remember yourself. You have navigated far from the paternal home, and now you inhabit a foreign land. But take heart. We are many, and our numbers are growing. Together, we will make this place our home.

You Are the Violin

We know precious little about how the human psyche really develops. We have our genetics, our astrology, our destiny, our collective unconscious, our inborn temperaments, our peer groups, our oceanic uterine memories. We have our families, our parents' love, nurturance, neglect and abuse. We grow up amid wars, revolutions, traditions and depressions. And somehow all of these things—biology, psychology, family, society, economy, spirituality and the unexplainable—come together like an orchestra to create the symphony of who we are, of who we may become.

To varying degrees throughout history, mothers have been held responsible for our children's psyches, for their behavior and for their overall well-being. If something went wrong in the symphony, it was Mom who, like a lousy conductor, took the blame for the bad reviews.

In an extreme example of mother-blaming in the 1950s, some terribly scientific studies labeled mothers of individual schizophrenic patients "schizogenic," and even though researchers knew that most of these mothers also had children who were not schizophrenic, the mothers were left with themselves to blame.

Recently, with advances in the fields of genetics and genetic engineering, psychological problems once blamed on nurture—moms, that is— were suddenly blamed on genes. Terribly scientific studies started popping up everywhere. This trend was a welcome one. Too many generations of mothers who were doing their best had been scapegoated. Our genes, I'm sure, are doing the best they can, too. But as far as we know, genes do not have the same capacity for guilt as mothers do. At least our genes won't keep themselves up at night thinking, "Where did I go wrong? I shouldn't have mutated!"

But I take these new genetic revelations with a few grains of salt. More recently, the focus has begun to shift again, this time toward environmental culprits, like peer interactions.

It would be nice, of course, if there were a single cause for all our problems, and one for all our promise, but I've yet to see a terribly scientific study that convinced me of that. Mothers are destiny. Genes are destiny. Astrology is destiny. Geography is destiny. Peers are destiny. Economy is destiny. Destiny is destiny sometimes. And all these things come together to make us who we are.

If our—and our children's—psyches are symphonies, remember that you are not the conductor. You are not even the whole string section. You are, let's say, the violin. This is not to suggest that your efforts are incidental. When I was ten I played the violin in the All City Orchestra. When I screwed up big time, I could wreck a whole movement with my screeching. When I played well, my part could be heard, followed, appreciated. But when, on occasion, I just moved my bow up and down with the others, careful not to let it touch the strings because I'd gotten distracted watching a certain African cellist who was the love of my young life, no one really noticed, except for the blonde girl with little round glasses who sat next to me, and she did her best, I think, to cover for my lapses.

Cry

On the way home from dropping Maia off at school on a cold, bright morning last winter, I ducked into a church to collect my thoughts. The place was empty, stone quiet, and filled with that light only stained glass and generations of reverence can create. I sat silently for about forty minutes, counting my breaths. Just as I was about to get up and leave, a young woman rushed in, looking even more stressed than I had when I arrived. She took no notice of me as she quickly tip-toed down the aisle and past the altar. She knelt before a stone statue of Mary and wept. She cried there for five minutes—not more than ten, anyway—and then she rose calmly and floated out of the church.

The spiritual teacher Mata Amritanandamayi, the Divine Mother Ammachi, has said that "crying to God for five minutes is worth an hour of meditation."

Meditation has become popular in Western countries in part because in order to reap its benefits, we do not have to believe in God. Neither do we have to believe in God, or in Mary, or in Ammachi, to cry. It's enough that we believe in our own experience. My experience is that Ammachi, and the woman weeping to Mary, and all the mothers around the world who cry, are right.

Now when I do not have time to meditate, when I feel too tightly wound to relax and concentrate, I find that five minutes of crying has the same effects. I think of my friend Wendy and her Pacific Ocean full of mothers' tears. Not so sad. It is a short cut to the calm that comes after a good, long hour of quiet meditation.

Sometimes we think of crying as losing control, as wimpy, as weak, as vulnerable, as crazy. Please join me in saying, *fuck that*. Being forever in control is overrated. There is no strength without letting go, without emptying out, without admitting how much we endure.

Not long ago, on a still Saturday night, I cried for six hours in a lover's arms. I realize this behavior could be seen as a certifiable acute depressive episode. And maybe it was. I prefer to think of it as a three-day meditation retreat for those of us who don't have the three days—a meditation retreat for the girl on the go. I highly recommend it.

Pray

Parenthood teaches—forces?—prayer. Please God don't let him stop breathing in his crib, you say now, and in no time at all he'll be off in Zimbabwe and you'll be saying, Don't let him get cerebral malaria or fall off his moto and need a transfusion of AIDS-contaminated blood or fail to see in time the next cobra that shows up in his kitchen.

NANCY MAIRS, *Ordinary Time*

When Maia was small, it was not "parenting" books that sustained me, but books of faith. One was a limited-edition, long-out-of-print volume on English churches. It was little, black and white, filled with psalms and pictures of old churches and rose gardens. Made with love and reverence, it was one of those books that are more than the sum of their parts. Regrettably, I sold it with a pile of other books to pay an electricity bill the winter Maia turned two. But even if I could remember the title or the author's name, I probably wouldn't be able to find it again. The closest approximations I have come across since are Marianne Williamson's *Illuminata* and Gabriele Uhlein's *Meditations with Hildegaard of Bingen*.

Those first two years of Maia's life were a sweet time for me, but they were also a lonely time. Often at night, after she'd gone to sleep and I couldn't bring myself to do any more school work, I'd sit down at my kitchen table, turn on a little lamp whose shade was painted with flowers, and read the psalms to myself.

I was raised in a rebel Catholic tradition by a priest who gave up the rigidity of the Church for my mother, so I am naturally drawn to Catholic images and prayers. They do not hold for me any of the oppressive connotations they are imbued with in so many Catholic schools and homes. Instead they remind me of the Sundays I spent watching my stepfather at the pulpit and the strange light that surrounded him there. He had endured much nonsense from the Roman Catholic Church—and finally excommunication—but he still loved Mary's Jewish refugee family as his own, still saw God in every river, mountain and reed on this green earth and once, when I was eight years old and preoccupied with my fate, had sat me down in a forest clearing and promised me there was no hell except those of our own making.

Those who have experienced a more oppressive religious upbringing often need to turn to new traditions or to the secular practices of meditation and relaxation to find solace. This is as it should be. Much has been written into all the great religions of the world (and even more has been edited out) for the purpose of keeping women and poor people in our places. Even in that sweet book on English churches, I had to resist the passages that encouraged self-sacrifice. I had to learn to disregard prayers and psalms and any songs to God that included the suggestion that I should give and give of myself, that the time for repose comes with death. That's nonsense. Any prayer worth the parchment it's written on is a work of poetry. And whether we call the poet a medium or a prophet or a saint, he was, first and foremost, a poet. And every poet who ever has been and ever will be, took much time for repose on this earth. She had a quiet space—even if that space was only a patch of grass on the convent grounds, a corner of her apartment or a seat on a commuter train.

Our spirituality should empower us. It should make us feel better about our lives. It should be useful to us here and now. And we should be wary of any heroine who sounds suspiciously like a doormat.

I'll tell you a story. I think it's meant to be a joke. Jesus was kicking back in heaven one afternoon, and he noticed that there seemed to be a lot of riffraff milling around. A punk rocker here, a militant feminist there. Jesus went to see Saint Peter about this. "You slacking off, man?" he wanted to know. "You can't just let *anyone* in here."

"I have to tell you," Saint Peter said to Jesus cautiously. "It's not me. It's your mom. She's been letting them in through the back door."

Whatever traditions our faith is rooted in, I know very few mothers who do not pray, at least in secret.

The Maternal Feminist Agenda

Here's a conversation I had with Maia recently:

    Her: I feel like you do too many jobs.

    Me: I *do* do too many jobs.

    Her: I know. That's what I feel.

    Me: What are we going to do about it?

    Her: I don't know. Maybe I can help you with some of the stuff. Like dishes. I like doing dishes.

    Me: Cool.

And a week later (while doing dishes):

    Her: I feel like we do too many jobs.

    Me: We *do* do too many jobs.

    Her: I know. That's what I feel.

    Me: What are we going to do about it?

    Her: I don't know. Maybe we can eat out more often.

    Me: *Hmmm—*

In the spirit of "what are we going to do about it?" and of Susie Bright's idea for a Million Mama March on Washington, I asked a bunch of shit-kicking mamas to weigh in with their top agenda items for the mama-revolution. Here are the highlights:

INGA

First and foremost, we need women to band together around the concept that all mothers are working mothers! We've let them pit us against each other—it's the ol' "divide and conquer" thing. We need to take responsibility for ourselves, each other and each other's children.

MONIKA

Mamás who bust butt and stay home need to be considered just as valuable as those who bust butt and work outside the home.

ANNE

We need high-quality affordable daycare now. Daycare includes infant care, toddler care, preschool, elementary school (with after-school programs), middle school (with after-school programs) and high school (with, you guessed it, after-school programs). This is my number one source of anxiety as a parent.

JENNIFER

We need sane gun control laws.

DANA

We need a tangible village: Mamas working outside the home should get subsidized for our daycare/educational solution of choice. Meaning: twelve thousand dollars per year for the grandmama, neighbor or home-school co-op,

*plus twenty-five hundred dollars per year for artistic/
passionate pursuits. Any man or woman who chooses to
stay home from a successful or imagined career in order
to take care of the babes gets thirty-five thousand dollars
per year and a burn-out relief allowance for periodic
reprieve. It's time we admitted that going it alone is a
burn-out job just like police work and fire fighting: Mamas
should get full retirement after twenty years of service.*

LAURA

*Survival. We all need food, shelter, health care and
clothing. We must do whatever it takes to ensure that no
child goes hungry, no matter whose toes get stepped on.*

SIERRA

*Diapers cost too much. HMOs suck. Teen mothers and
welfare mothers are demonized as witches. Apathy and
frustration are hard to avoid, but avoid them! Stage
public nurse-ins every place where feeding our babies is
considered "obscene." Demand child- and family-friendly
environments everywhere!*

NANCI

*What we need is true sharing of the roles of parenting if
there is a partner involved. No more glorifying Dad or
partner for taking the kids on a "special outing." True
equality.*

MICHAEL

We need a poor people's campaign to change the face of

America: Give communities control of police and educa-
tion, ban all nuclear weapons and nuclear power,
demobilize U.S. troops and bases around the world,
decriminalize drugs, support women's right to control
their own bodies, guarantee child support/welfare,
demand a worldwide jubilee forgiveness of debt, protect
labor organizing and workplace rights, reverse deforesta-
tion and global warming and decolonize the biosphere!

DONI-MARIE

We need to make motherhood a hot topic—the issue of the
species. Otherwise we'll just have to go on a breeding
strike. We have to muster up some self-respect and gain
some visibility. We need to be the bold new role models of
motherhood beyond Betty Crocker and Super Career Mom.

And that, my friends, is the maternal feminist agenda. It's wide open for additions and adaptations. The important thing is to be gentle with yourself and with your family so that we can all live soulfully in this incomplete revolution— saving the rage to fuel social transformation. Imagine if we took all of the energy we spend beating ourselves up for our failure to adjust to this insane world where mothers work double shifts and shoulder the blame for everything from individual children's bad behavior to global economic crises—imagine that we turned that energy outward and used to it make this world our home.

Revolution in Cyberspace

Last winter the small Internet publishing company that had run hipmama.com for more than two years informed me that the gig was up—they didn't have the money to keep the site online. They'd have to pull the plug in two days. I immediately decided I could run the thing myself. But reality hit a few minutes later. I didn't even know HTML, the language to publish on the Web. I simply couldn't do it. I'd keep editing and publishing the print version of the zine—the online community would have to settle for my small stone. The Web site was important to me, and I knew it was important to the mamas who hung out on the discussion boards, but I rationalized that it hadn't been there a few years earlier. . . they could do without it again.

We quickly posted news of the imminent demise of hipmama.com.

The first responses I got from community members were panicked and accusatory. Like, "How could you?"

I explained I didn't have the time to run the site, didn't have the money to pay the site's bills, didn't have the hardware, the software, the Internet know-how, *anything.*

The community's tone changed. Suddenly it was like, "Why didn't you *say* so?"

In a moment I can only now, in hindsight, pinpoint, the whole structure of the conversation changed. Folks stopped talking to me, and they started talking to each other. It was like the best readings or book signings I've done—the ones where, in the end, I can slip out the back door unnoticed as the mamas who came to hear me start looking around the room at each other and then start organizing and exchanging phone numbers. It was an organic anarchy without power struggles or any other weirdness. This site was their support system, after all, it was their room in the dark, their community and their consciousness-raising group. They weren't going to let some madwoman in Oakland cut them off just because she didn't know HTML. Within forty-eight hours, as I sat back with my jaw hanging open, these women pooled the needed funds, located a new server and found discussion software. Bee Lavender, a renegade public administrator, home-schooling mama and long-time community member took over as editor. Other women volunteered as designers, writers and bookkeepers. They came up with a kick-ass new design and looked around the independent publishing world to find a way to pay the bills. They figured out how to make the business work in a tangible way. They didn't just keep the site up without interruption, they poured their passionate energy into doing the job in a way that would actively improve and support the community.

A mama like me can start something, but, if it's any good, pretty soon it will take on a life of its own. Before the revolution in cyberspace, I figured I had a quirky little project that people enjoyed. It wasn't until the site's near-death experience that I saw clearly that *Hip Mama* actually had little to do with me. Sure, it resembles my original vision for the zine, but it is no longer just mine. Hell, "Hip Mama" no longer refers to a zine at all. From the mamas' mouths:

> *It describes a woman who has chosen to become a mother but still retain her own personality.*

> *[The community] has filled me with joy, pissed me off, saddened me, soothed me and educated me.*

> *It's the most effective, organically-grown community I have ever been a part of.*

> *I am pretty new to this community, but for me it's become a place where I can come and spend some time with women who enrich my life, make me think, open my eyes to other lifestyles and remind me of the beauty in the everyday occurrences that make up my life.*

The audience is phenomenal (and huge!)—stretching from Oakland to Portland to New York to the United Arab Emirates to South Africa to Hong Kong and back again. We are strong, progressive and eclectic. The site features fine journalism and honest personal essays. The discussion board has made a difference in real, practical ways. People meet in person and form support networks. Women leave abusive relationships. We learn from vibrant debates that we can

221

tolerate difference. We learn that if we take the time to talk, to listen to each other and to take care of ourselves, we can silence the voices that have trained us to fail. We can decolonize our imaginations.

Motherhood is not what we thought, that's true. It is more difficult, more heart-wrenching and more delightful than we ever dreamed. But we had children because mothering is good for the soul. And we learn that instead of selling off pieces of that soul for promises of stability and perfection, we can keep fighting to change the world, and we can also be gentle with ourselves and with our children in the process.

I am in many ways freer as a mother than my mother was. She is in many ways freer as a mother than her mother was. But I imagine that my children and perhaps even my children's children will be grown before we have completely reinvented family and society so that they serve women as well as children and men, so that we can have kids, be swallowed in the mad-love of child-rearing, but also work, create, worship and love without feeling as if we have to do all these things simultaneously, at a break-neck pace that doesn't allow us to savor any of it.

We are living in the midst of an incomplete revolution, but we can live here honestly. We can give our children reasonable limits; we can nurture their innate talents; we can keep our promises—regardless. We can *want little, need less. Forget the rules. Be untroubled.* And we can do all this at our own pace, one that allows us to savor all of it.

Six Early-Morning Dreams

I.   (Some years ago) The apartment is on fire. I grab a favorite out-of-print book, put on a flannel robe and run outside, relieved to have escaped. I hear the fire engines circling. The sirens sound near but then recede, close but then further away, as if they are lost. Suddenly, I remember the baby. Running back upstairs, I burn my feet. In the thick smoke, I cannot find her. I hear her singing a soft lullaby, oblivious in her crib, but I cannot reach her, the baby who is not yet firmly attached to me.

II.   I am getting an Athenian owl tattooed on my back. I am behind myself, watching the artist move her needle across my skin. The owl suddenly takes flight. "Damn," she says. "That always happens."

III.   I do radio interview after radio interview after radio interview. All day. Different hosts. Different stations. Different cities. My girlfriend calls to tell me it's getting boring. "It's pure documentary now," I tell her. "You didn't even challenge that last guy," she complains. "He's the most conservative voice on radio." I hadn't noticed. We spoke of vegetable gardening.

IV.   I wake up, and Maia is painting the apartment with murals of fish, flowers, oceans and strange translucent birds. She asks me to help her build a scaffolding so that she can do the ceiling. We build it out of car parts and suitcases. "We're never going to get our deposit back," I mumble as I crawl back into bed.

V.   Maia and I are at my grandmother's house on the beach. The tide has risen so that the house is completely surrounded by the ocean. My grandmother is inside the house. She does not notice the water outside. She is talking to my cousin about remodeling. My daughter and I are floating around outside the house in rubber inner tubes.

VI.   I again dream the apartment is on fire. I roll out of bed easily and crawl into my daughter's room. "Come on, girl-child," I whisper. "We won't lose much." And we slither out a back door I have never seen before. No sirens circle on this night. We watch in awe as the building burns, casting an electric red glow into the sky. We turn away from the fire then and fly, slow and awkward like young owls, up into the branches of an old oak tree. And we wait there.

The Marathon Monks

In Japan, Tendai Buddhist monks run some twenty to fifty miles a day along the snowy slopes of Mount Hiei. They do this for one hundred consecutive days, rising at one-thirty in the morning to begin their route. They carry with them a sword and a rope to remind them to commit suicide if they fail. I imagine they entertain great doubt in the beginning, waking in the night, thinking: *Maybe those corporate suckers back in Tokyo had it right all along.*

Over a period of seven years, the marathon monks go on ten such hundred-day runs, covering some twenty-two thousand miles in all. At the end of the seven years, they go without food or sleep for nine days. Those who survive the entire ordeal are considered living Buddhas, wise and awake.

Of course, you cannot join the order if you are a mother.

You wouldn't have to.

Works Cited

Allison, Dorothy. *Two or Three Things I Know for Sure.* New York: Dutton, 1995.

Amritaswarupananda, Swami, Ramakrishna Chaitanya and Neal Rosner. *For My Children: Selected Teachings Of Divine Mother Ammachi.* Castro Valley: Mata Amritanandamayi Center, 1994.

Blake, William. *Songs of Experience.* New York: Milton, 1927.

Budapest, Z. "Daughter of the Goddess: Interview with Z. Budapest." By Susan Bridle. *What Is Enlightenment?* 10, no. 2 (Fall/Winter 1996): 65-71.

Budapest, Z. *Summoning the Fates: A Woman's Guide to Destiny.* New York: Harmony Books, 1998.

Cavanaugh, Tim. "Totalizing Quality Management." *Mother Jones* 23, no. 1 (Jan-Feb 1998): 71.

Chödrön, Pema. *When Things Fall Apart: Heart Advice for Difficult Times.* Boston: Shambhala Publications, 1997.

Covey, Stephen R. *The Seven Habits of Highly Effective Families: Building a Beautiful Family Culture in a Turbulent World.* New York: Golden Books, 1997.

Day, Dorothy. *Meditations.* New York: Newman Press, 1970.

Estés, Clarissa Pinkola. *Women Who Run with the Wolves: Myths and Stories of the Wild Woman Archetype.* New York: Ballantine Books, 1995.

Ezzo, Gary, and Robert Buckman, M.D. *On Becoming Babywise.* Sisters, OR: Multnomah Publishers, 1998.

Field, Joanna. *A Life of One's Own.* Los Angeles: J.P. Tarcher, Inc., 1981.

Fisher, Carrie. Quoted in Philip Zimmerman, *The Paz Pages* (Web site). http://www.apriori.net/~paz/quotes.html, June 1999.

Frantz, Marge. Quoted in Dena Taylor (editor), *Feminist Parenting: Struggles, Triumphs & Comic Interludes* (Freedom, Calif.: Crossing Press, 1994), 43.

Fraser, Clara. *Revolution, She Wrote.* Seattle: Red Letter Press, 1998

Gilman, Susan Jane. "Five Ways to Recover from Stupid Health Advice." *Hues* 4, no. 2 (Spring 1998): 10-11.

Goldberg, Natalie. *Long Quiet Highway: Waking Up in America.* New York: Bantam, 1994.

Graves, A.J. *Woman in America; being an examination into the moral and intellectual condition of American female society.* New York: Harper and Brothers, 1843.

Graves, Robert. *Greek Myths: Complete Edition.* New York: Penguin Books, 1992.

Greer, Germaine. *The Whole Woman.* New York: A.A. Knopf, 1999.

Hurston, Zora Neale. *Their Eyes Were Watching God* (Perennial Classic). New York: HarperCollins, 1999.

Kennedy, Pagan. *Pagan Kennedy's Living: The Handbook for Maturing Hipsters.* New York: St. Martin's Griffin, 1997.

Lazarre, Jane. *The Mother Knot.* Durham, NC: Duke University Press, 1997.

Lazarre, Jane. Quoted in Tillie Olsen, *Silences* (New York: Delta, 1989), 211.

Lerner, Harriet. *The Mother Dance: How Children Change Your Life.* New York: Harper Collins, 1998.

MacRae, George W. (translator). "The Thunder, Perfect Mind." *The Gnosis Archive* (Web site), http://www.webcom.com/gnosis/naghamm/thunder.html. From James M. Robinson (editor), *The Nag Hammadi Library* (San Francisco: HarperCollins, 1990).

Mairs, Nancy. *Ordinary Time: Cycles in Marriage, Faith, and Renewal.* Boston: Beacon Press, 1993.

Nietzsche, Friedrich. *Thus Spoke Zarathustra*. New York: Penguin Classics, 1978.

Nin, Anaïs. *The Novel of the Future*. New York: MacMillan, 1968.

Nin, Anïs, and Evelyn J. Hinz (editor). *A Woman Speaks: The Lectures, Seminars and Interviews of Anaïs Nin.* Athens, Ohio: Ohio University Press, 1976.

Olsen, Tillie. *Silences.* New York: Delta, 1989.

Plath, Sylvia. Quoted in Tillie Olsen, *Silences* (New York: Delta, 1989), 36.

Phillips, Utah. "Natural Resources." *The Moscow Hold & Other Stories.* Compact Disc. Red House Records, 1999.

Rich, Adrienne. *Of Woman Born: Motherhood as Experience and Institution.* New York: W.W. Norton & Company, 1995.

Rukeyser, Muriel. *The Life of Poetry.* New York: Current Books, 1949.

Sheehy, Gail. *Passages.* New York: Bantam, 1984.

Shlain, Leonard. *The Alphabet Versus the Goddess: The Conflict Between Word and Image.* New York: Penguin, 1999.

Stein, Gertrude. Quoted in Sophy Burnham, *For Writers Only* (New York: Ballantine, 1994), 28.

Stowe, Harriet Beecher. Quoted in Tillie Olsen, *Silences* (New York: Delta, 1979), 204.

Tzu, Lao. *Tao Te Ching.* Translated by Ursula K. Le Guin. Boston: Shambhala Books, 1997.

Walker, Alice. *Anything We Love Can Be Saved: A Writer's Activism.* New York: Random House, 1997.

Willard, Frances. Quoted in Mary Frances Berry, *The Politics of Parenthood: Child Care, Women's Rights, and the Myth of the Good Mother* (New York: Viking, 1993), 68.

Acknowledgments

Thanks and blessings to Maia, Jennie Goode and Seal Press, Ophira Edut, Bee Lavender, Leslie, Nanci Olesen, my family and the *Hip Mama* and girl-mom.com communities.

About the Author

Ariel Gore is the founder and editor of *Hip Mama*, an award-winning zine covering the culture and politics of motherhood. She has degrees from Mills College and the University of California at Berkeley and lives with her daughter in beautiful Oakland, California.

Selected Seal Press Titles

Adiós, Barbie: Young Women Write About Body Image and Identity edited by Ophira Edut. $14.95, 1-58005-016-6. Essays filled with honesty and humor by women who have chosen to ignore, subvert or redefine the dominant beauty standard.

The Adoption Reader: Birthmothers, Adoptive Mothers and Adopted Daughters Tell Their Stories edited by Susan Wadia-Ells. $16.95, 1-878067-65-6. With eloquence and conviction, more than thirty birthmothers, adoptive mothers and adopted daughters explore the many faces of adoption.

Cunt: A Declaration of Independence by Inga Muscio. $14.95, 1-58005-015-8. An ancient title of respect for women, "cunt" now careens toward the heart of every woman as an expletive. This book gives women the tools to claim "cunt" as a positive and powerful force in their lives.

The Lesbian Parenting Book: A Guide to Creating Families and Raising Children by D. Merilee Clunis and G. Dorsey Green. $16.95, 1-878067-68-0. This practical and readable book covers a wide range of parenting topics as well as issues specifically relevant to lesbian families.

Reunion: A Year in Letters Between a Birthmother and Her Daughter, by Katie Hern and Ellen McGarry Carlson. $16.95, 1-58005-030-1. The first book co-written by an adopted daughter and her birthmother, blending the real-life experiences of adoption with an inspiring story of love and acceptance.

The Single Mother's Companion: Essays and Stories by Women edited by Marsha Leslie. $12.95, 1-878067-56-7. In their own words, the single mothers in this landmark collection explore both the joys and the difficult realities of raising children alone.

Wild Child: Girlhoods in the Counterculture edited by Chelsea Cain. $16.00, 1-58005-031-X. In this collection of wise and irreverent essays, daughters of the hippie generation reflect on the effects of a counterculture childhood.

Seal Press publishes many books of fiction and nonfiction by women writers. If you are unable to obtain a Seal Press title from a bookstore or would like a free catalog of our books, please order from us directly by calling 1-800-754-0271. Visit our website at www.sealpress.com.